I0868539

What It's Worth: Valuing Residential and Commercial Construction Companies

A BVR SPECIAL REPORT

Pasquale Rafanelli, CPA/ABV, ASA, CVA, CBA, CFE, MAFF, CDFA®

BVR
What It's Worth

111 SW Columbia Street, Suite 750, Portland, OR 97201-5814
503-479-8200 • www.bvresources.com

BVR

What It's Worth

Copyright © 2020 by Business Valuation Resources, LLC (BVR). All rights reserved.
Printed in the United States of America.

No part of this publication may be reprinted, reproduced, stored in a retrieval system or transmitted in any form or by any means, electronic, mechanical, photocopying, recording, scanning or otherwise, except as permitted under Sections 107 or 108 of the 1976 United States Copyright Act, without either the prior written permission of the Publisher or authorization through payment of the appropriate per copy fee to the Publisher. Requests for permission should be addressed to the Permissions Department, Business Valuation Resources, LLC, 111 SW Columbia Street, Suite 750, Portland, OR 97201-5814; (503) 479-8200; fax (503) 291-7955; permissions@bvresources.com.

Information contained in this book has been obtained by Business Valuation Resources from sources believed to be reliable. However, neither Business Valuation Resources nor its authors guarantee the accuracy or completeness of any information published herein and neither Business Valuation Resources nor its authors shall be responsible for any errors, omissions, or damages arising out of use of this information. This work is published with the understanding that Business Valuation Resources and its authors are supplying information but are not attempting to render business valuation or other professional services. If such services are required, the assistance of an appropriate professional should be sought.

Editor: Pasquale Rafanelli

Publisher: Sarah Andersen

Managing Editor: Monique Nijhout-Rowe

Senior Copy Editor: David Solomon

Desktop Editor: Warren Simons

Chair and CEO: David Foster

President: Lucretia Lyons

Chief Revenue Officer: Lisa McInturff

Print/PDF ISBN: 978-1-62150-166-4

EPUB ISBN: 978-1-62150-167-1

LCCN: 2019941696

Table of Contents

Introduction

When looking to appraise or value both residential and commercial construction companies, there are many unique factors to consider that set this industry apart from others. There is the seasonality of the business, which often means cash flow can be very low to nonexistent in the winter and pick up in the spring and summer months. Also, companies must follow specific requirements to be able to bid on contracts from federal, state, and local governments, as well as contracted set-asides for businesses owned by women, minorities, and veterans. There are even special rules for determining what qualifies for these ownership types.

In this BVR special report, *What It's Worth: Valuing Residential and Commercial Construction Companies,* you'll get advice from a top expert who values both residential and commercial companies and works with this industry daily. You'll read a case study of a construction company for the purposes of outlining several of the factors that go into the valuation of a privately held business. You'll learn the specifics of how the key issues can influence value. Further, the report provides valuation multiples that can help you benchmark the value of a construction company.

Whether you're looking to buy, sell, or value a residential or commercial construction business, it's important to consider construction company valuation from a number of different angles, from special considerations in valuing a construction company to how to cash out. This special report will help you do just that. After reading this report, you'll see what builds value in residential and commercial construction companies.

Pasquale Rafanelli

Pasquale Rafanelli, CPA/ABV, ASA, CVA/CBA/MAFF, CFE, CDFA®
Empire Valuation Consultants

Editor's Biography

Pasquale Rafanelli, CPA/ABV, ASA, CVA/CBA/MAFF, CFE, CDFA®, is a senior manager at Empire Valuation Consultants. He has more than 13 years of experience providing business valuation, forensic accounting, and advisory services to closely held companies, attorneys, accountants, and financial professionals. He has performed valuations of business interests for a variety of purposes including, but not limited to, family law matters, estate and gift tax matters, business damages, corporate litigation, and shareholder disputes. Pasquale can be reached at prafanelli@empireal.com or 631-719-3222.

SECTION I:
VALUE DRIVERS AND VALUATION OF RESIDENTIAL AND NONRESIDENTIAL CONSTRUCTION COMPANIES

1. Opportunities for Business Appraisers to Value Residential and Nonresidential Construction Companies

By Pasquale Rafanelli

In many ways, the construction industry is no different from other industries in the sense that it faces constant changes and fluctuations over time. One recent example in which the construction industry hit a serious roadblock was when the economy crashed between 2008 and 2009. Ever since then, residential and commercial construction has been in a steady state of rebound.

Over the next five years, from 2019 to 2024, the global construction industry is expected to have good opportunities in the residential, nonresidential, and infrastructure industries. Global Construction Perspectives and Oxford Economics recently released their global benchmark study, which estimates that the construction industry is expected to grow at a compounded annual compounded annual growth rate (CAGR) of 3.9% and is forecasted to reach an estimated $15.5 trillion by 2030, with the United States, China, and India leading the way, accounting for approximately 57% of all global growth. People attribute this anticipated growth to many different factors including increasing housing starts and rising infrastructure due to increasing urbanization and the growing population.

Emerging trends also have a direct impact on the dynamics of the construction industry. The industry as a whole is seeing an increasing demand for:

- Green construction to reduce carbon footprint;
- Bridge lock-up device systems to enhance the life of structures;

- Building information systems for efficient building management; and
- The use of fiber-reinforced polymer composites for the rehabilitation of aging structures.

Let's take a look at some of the other more prominent trends and opportunities in the residential and nonresidential construction market place:

Residential Trends

- *Consolidation.* The easiest way for a company to enter new markets and strengthen its position in existing markets is to continue to grow through acquisitions. Larger firms, which stockpiled cash and land during the economic downturn, are looking to expand, especially as home values and buyer demand start to stabilize. A potential benefit in consolidations is that large homebuilders tend to enjoy economies of scale, with national purchasing power for materials and greater access to capital.
- *Nonhomebuilding services.* In today's market it is not uncommon for builders to branch off into other related fields such as:
    - Modular and manufactured housing;
    - Construction materials;
    - Commercial construction;
    - Mortgages; and
    - Insurance.

  Some builders have even established mortgage banking arms to provide financing for home buyers. This service typically focuses on the operations to originate mortgages and then to sell them to other investors.
- *High-tech homes.* We live in a high-tech world—one that is constantly changing—and builders are starting to respond to the current consumer demand by building more new houses with advanced data and other communication capabilities. Consumers raised on electronics and computers expect structured wiring that supports smart

home technologies such as learning thermostats and internet-enabled security and monitoring features.

- *Green construction.* Although a green home can cost more than a conventional house, some lenders are offering mortgage incentives for energy-efficient homes. Some of the green building innovations include:
    - More porous materials in walkways and patios to prevent erosion from rain runoff;
    - Engineered recycled lumber in building; and
    - The conversion of wood or drywall construction waste on-site into landscape mulch.
- *Millennials becoming homeowners.* Millennial home buyers, particularly those who have started families, are navigating toward more affordable residential areas that promise high job growth. The suburbs are successfully attracting first-time home buyers and younger individuals because these areas are typically much less expensive than those nearest major metro areas.
- *Internet marketing.* An active online presence can dramatically improve traffic to sales centers, increase conversion rates, and improve customer satisfaction by enabling builders to stay connected with customers through the entire home ownership cycle. With internet and mobile application technology, potential buyers can visit a number of different developments, view the types of models available, and take virtual tours through model homes. These sites also have the capability to allow buyers to apply for mortgages and insurance at their convenience.
- *Special-purpose housing developments.* The changing demographics of the U.S. population suggest that demand for second homes and retirement communities will increase. The large baby-boomer generation is now in its peak years of earning power and asset accumulation, potentially giving them the means to buy second homes for vacations. Further, this generation is in the age range for retirement in the next decade.
- *Multifamily and for-rent apartments.* High demand for apartments and condos has resulted in many traditionally single-family home builders turning to multifamily construction. In today's changing market, many people are unable to afford to buy a home or cannot qualify for a mortgage, which creates stronger demand for rental properties.

Builders are starting to follow the trend by increasing their presence in building apartment complexes and condo communities.

- *Need for repairs and retrofits.* The inventory of homes in the U.S. is aging. As a result, there is higher demand for major repairs and maintenance. According to the National Association of Home Builders, more than 65% of U.S. owner-occupied homes were built before 1990. These homes may be sold at lower prices but require extensive investments to update and repair them. As a result, residential construction contractors also may win more contracts to remodel and refurbish older homes. In addition, homebuilding slowed during the recession, creating a lack of new inventory, which has resulted in a pent-up demand for new homes. Residential builders that specialize in green and/or high-tech new construction will benefit long term as more people look to buy new homes in a market filled with old houses.

- *Competition from commercial builders.* More commercial builders are considering residential construction as an extension of their regular business, although residential construction requires different skills. While residential construction tends to have increased risks, it also offers higher margins than commercial work.

Nonresidential trends. While a lot of the trends are the same for residential and nonresidential construction, there are a few worth referencing below:

- *Design-build.* The growing design-build movement encourages collaborative project development in all phases of design and construction. Significant cost and schedule savings as well as increased quality can result from collaboration on technologically sophisticated projects.

- *Modular construction.* Permanent modular construction can enhance the speed and efficiency of project completion. Modular components can be built off-site in a factory or warehouse and are then transported and placed. Advancements in modular technology allows for more durable, versatile structures.

- *Urbanization.* The world's population is becoming increasingly concentrated in urban areas, a trend that drives demand for structures such as airports, office buildings, parking garages, restaurants, and shopping malls. According to the United Nations, in 2014, approximately 50% of the world's population resided in urban areas, and, by 2050, it is projected that more than 60% of the population will live in urban areas.

- *Green building.* As mentioned in the residential section above, demand is growing for environmentally friendly building, which includes construction materials, practices, and certification. According to the United Nations Environment Programme, buildings are responsible for more than 40% of global energy use and one-third of global greenhouse gas emissions. Construction companies with green building capabilities are positioned to benefit from increasing efforts in the commercial and government sectors to build and operate more environmentally friendly buildings.

- *Emerging markets.* Developing countries provide some of the greatest opportunities for construction expansion. According to Global Construction Perspectives and Oxford Economics, it is predicted that the U.S., China, and India will account for more than half of global construction growth between 2015 and 2030.

- *Mixed-use developments.* Construction of mixed-use developments that combine residential, office, and commercial spaces will likely increase as the population becomes more urbanized. Some city planners advocate for such projects because placing residents and workers closer to stores and restaurants can help reduce city traffic. Nonresidential construction firms may start to expand their building expertise through joint ventures or acquisitions to take advantage of mixed-use development demand.

- *Joint ventures.* As projects get bigger, on-time completion becomes more important to owners of construction firms. Costs for late completion, including penalties, rise disproportionately to actual construction costs. The larger scale and more complex projects lead to more joint ventures among construction companies, which can pool their expertise and financial resources in bidding for contracts and in implementation.

As discussed throughout this chapter, there are plenty of opportunities in the market for business owners to consider and take advantage of to grow their businesses. This, as a result, has increased the need for appraisers not only to play a pivotal role in providing valuation services for their clients, but also to act as their advisor and give them the help and tools they need to better position themselves in the market.

2. Special Considerations in Valuing Construction Companies

By Pasquale Rafanelli

Every industry has its own nuances and complex issues that one needs to consider when starting the valuation process. Understanding these issues and knowing how to properly apply them is just as important, if not more important, than knowing how to perform a valuation.

Accounting considerations. Construction contractors utilize various methods of accounting. For this reason, the valuation analyst needs to closely consider the type of accounting the company he or she is valuing utilizes because misunderstanding how the company does accounting can significantly impact its ultimate value.

The most significant accounting issue for construction contractors is the method of accounting for long-term contracts. While there are multiple methods of accounting, the four most common are:

- *Cash basis method.* Many construction contractors are small businesses, for which the use of cash basis accounting is the common method. In cash basis accounting, earnings are recognized when cash is received from customers and expenses are recognized when cash is paid to the vendors. This poses an added layer of complexity when performing a valuation as valuators should, when possible, convert the cash basis financials to accrual basis financials. It is important for an appraiser to convert from cash basis to accrual basis because the cash basis method of accounting does not measure the true revenue and earnings power of the business and instead measures how creative or aggressive the owners were in minimizing their taxes. Therefore, using the cash basis accounting method would not provide the appraiser with the accurate net income or cash flows, and, as a result, the appraiser would arrive at an inaccurate value for the business.

- *Accrual basis method.* Under the accrual basis of accounting, a company records the revenues when earned and the expenses are recorded when incurred regardless of whether or not cash was exchanged. This method includes accounts on the balance sheet that we would not see under the cash basis method such as accounts receivable and accounts payable. These are important accounts to consider to arrive at the true operating cash flow within the context of a valuation.

For construction companies, in particular, there are two primary accrual basis methods that one can use:

- *Completed-contract method.* Under the completed-contract method, revenues and related costs are recognized in the period in which the contract is completed. General and administrative expenses not allocated to a particular project are recognized as incurred. This method can be useful for contractors who have projects that last less than a year. The critical thing to remember is that, under generally accepted accounting principles (GAAP), revenues and expenses need to be matched and recorded in the appropriate period. By recording revenues when the project is complete and expenses when incurred, the items may not match the appropriate period. But, if the contract is less than a calendar/fiscal year, regardless of when the revenues are recorded, they will match with the expenses as originally recorded.

- *Percentage of completion method.* The revenues and costs for each project are tracked separately under the percentage of completion method. The actual costs incurred are compared to the estimated costs to develop a percentage of completion, which is then applied to the total contract revenues to determine the amount of revenue to recognize. This method is useful for construction contractors who engage in projects that span a year or more.

The following examples demonstrate how accounting is done utilizing the different methods.

At the beginning of 2016, Salvatore Construction Co. received a contract to build an office building for $5 million. Salvatore will construct the building according to specifications the buyer provided, and the project is estimated to take three years to complete. According to the contract, Salvatore will bill the buyer in installments over the construction period according to a prearranged schedule (see Exhibit 1).

Completed contract method. Under the completed contract method, we would not record the revenues until the project is completed, which, in this case, is three years. Therefore, in 2018, we would make the revenue recognition entry shown in Exhibit 2.

Exhibit 1. Construction Company Prearranged Billing Schedule

	2016 ($)	2017 ($)	2018 ($)
Construction costs incurred during the year	1,500,000	1,000,000	1,600,000
Construction costs incurred in prior years	-	1,500,000	2,500,000
Cumulative actual construction costs	1,500,000	2,500,000	4,100,000
Estimated cost to complete at end of year	2,250,000	1,500,000	-
Total estimated actual construction costs	3,750,000	4,000,000	4,100,000
Billings made during the year	1,200,000	2,000,000	1,800,000
Cash collections during the year	1,000,000	1,400,000	2,600,000

Exhibit 2. Completed Contract Accounting Method Revenue Recognition

		2018 ($)	
		Debit	Credit
Construction in progress		900,000	
Cost of construction		4,100,000	
	Revenue from long-term contracts		5,000,000

As shown in Exhibit 2, since the project spanned over more than one year, we did not properly match the revenues and expenses in the appropriate year, which distorts the business's net income for prospective users. As a result, this method is typically only appropriate for short-term contracts that are less than one year and take place within the same calendar/fiscal year.

The advantage of the completed contract method is that it normally achieves the maximum deferral of taxes.

The disadvantages of the completed contract method are:

- The books and records do not show clear information on operations;
- Income can be bunched into a year when many jobs are completed; and
- Losses on contracts are not deductible until the contracts are completed.

Percentage of completion method. Using the same scenario for Salvatore Construction Co., let's look at how the entry would be made under the percentage of completion method.

The percentage of completion method records revenues over time according to the percentage of project completion. The formula is as follows:

Revenue recognized this period =
(total estimated revenue × percentage completed to date) - revenue recognized in prior periods.

Exhibit 3 shows how revenue would be recognized under the percentage of completion method.

Exhibit 4 shows the calculation used to arrive at the percentage of completion.

Exhibit 5 shows the yearly journal entries that would be made under the percentage of completion method.

There are some advantages to using the percentage of completion method:

- It provides better matching of income and expenses; and
- It gives a more accurate picture of your financial position.

Exhibit 3. Percentage of Completion Method Revenue Recognition*

	2016 ($)	2017 ($)	2018 ($)
Contract price	5,000,000	5,000,000	5,000,000
Multiplied by percentage of completion	40.0%	62.5%	100.0%
Cumulative revenue to recognize	2,000,000	3,125,000	5,000,000
Revenue to recognize per year	2,000,000	1,125,000	1,875,000

* Please note: The cumulative revenue to recognize is based on the percentage of completions each year. In this example, we recognize 40% of revenue in 2016, 62.5% of revenue in 2017, and 100% of the revenue by 2018.

Exhibit 4. Calculation to Determine Percentage of Completion

	2016 ($)	2017 ($)	2018 ($)
Actual costs to date	1,500,000	2,500,000	4,100,000
Divided by total costs (estimated costs + actual costs)	3,750,000	4,000,000	4,100,000
Percentage of completion	40.0%	62.5%	100.0%

Exhibit 5. Journal Entry for Percentage of Completion Method

		2016 ($)	
		Debit	Credit
Construction in progress		500,000	
Cost of construction		1,500,000	
	Revenue from long-term contracts		2,000,000
		2017 ($)	
		Debit	Credit
Construction in progress		125,000	
Cost of construction		1,000,000	
	Revenue from long-term contracts		1,125,000
		2018 ($)	
		Debit	Credit
Construction in progress		275,000	
Cost of construction		1,600,000	
	Revenue from long-term contracts		1,875,000

The main disadvantage to this method is its complexity and ability to properly estimate future costs of the job over the project's life.

Losses. Another issue encountered in accounting for a construction project is when to record a loss. There are two types of losses:

- *Periodic loss.* This occurs when there is a loss in the current period but the project is projected to be profitable at completion. When using the percentage of completion method and a periodic loss occurs, the loss is recorded as a credit to the construction in progress account. Conversely, if we are using the completed contract method, no entry is made as no revenue has been recognized.

- *Overall loss.* This occurs when there is a loss in the current period and the project is projected to be a loss at completion. When using the percentage of completion method and an overall loss occurs, we back out any gross profits recognized in prior periods and also recognize the overall loss. Then we can back into the cost of construction by adding the amount of the loss recognized to the amount of revenue recognized. Exhibit 6 illustrates how this is done.

Exhibit 6. Recording an Overall Loss Within the Percentage of Completion Method

	2016 ($)	2017 ($)	2018 ($)
Construction costs incurred during the year	1,500,000	1,260,000	2,440,000
Construction costs incurred in prior years	-	1,500,000	2,760,000
Cumulative actual construction costs	1,500,000	2,760,000	5,200,000
Estimated cost to complete at end of year	2,250,000	2,340,000	-
Total estimated actual construction costs	3,750,000	5,100,000	5,200,000
	Over Time	**Upon Completion**	
Gross profit (loss) recognized:			
2016	500,000	-	
2017	(600,000)	(100,000)	
2018	(100,000)	(100,000)	
2016			
Revenue recognized	2,000,000		
Cost of construction	(1,500,000)		
Gross profit	500,000		
2017			
Revenue recognized to date	2,706,000		
Revenue recognized in 2016	(2,000,000)		
Revenue recognized		706,000	
Cost of construction (PLUG)		(1,306,000)	
Loss		(600,000)	
2018			
Revenue recognized to date	5,000,000		
Revenue recognized in 2016	(2,706,000)		
Revenue recognized		2,294,000	
Cost of construction (PLUG)		(2,394,000)	
Loss		(100,000)	

Losses using the completed contract method. One important rule to remember when using the completed contract method is that, even though the recognition of revenues is delayed until the project is completed, if an overall loss is anticipated for the contract, that loss must be recognized in the first period in which it is anticipated.

This adds a layer of complexity when performing a valuation for a company that uses the completed contracts method as it requires the appraiser to critically analyze all ongoing contracts to determine whether any projects are forecasted to have an overall loss, and, if so, to ensure that they are properly recorded as not to skew the value of the business.

Underbillings and overbillings. The amount a contractor bills to a client rarely matches the amount that should be recognized based on the percentage of completion method. This disparity happens because billing cycles do not always match the reporting periods. For example, the process of obtaining approval for a change order may delay the actual billing of that change order. In addition, billing policies and procedures may be different than what the percentage of completion method implied. These disparities are classified as one of two things:

- Costs and estimated earnings in excess of billings also known as underbillings, which are reported on the balance sheet as a current asset; and
- Billings in excess of costs and estimated earnings are also known as overbillings, which are reported on the balance sheet as a current liability.

Retentions. Another accounting issue for construction contractors is retentions. Retentions are amounts the customer holds back or retains from each billing until the completion of a project. The owner of a project may withhold retention from the general contractor. In turn, the general contractor may withhold retention from the subcontractors.

The rule of thumb on the retention amount is typically between 5% and 10% of each billing. Once a project is completed to the customer's satisfaction, the retention is released. The purpose of the retention is to provide incentive to the contractor to complete the project to the satisfaction of the customer.

Income tax issues. Valuators need to consider several income tax issues when analyzing the financials of a construction company. These issues are summarized below.

Completed contract method. According to Reg. 1.451-3[d] [5], the completed contract method may be used for tax purposes, but only under a limited set of circumstances. This makes sense based on our earlier discussion, especially if the project spans more than a one-year period. This is important for analysts to consider in their valuation as using this method does not properly reflect income and expenses in the period they were earned or incurred, unless the project starts and ends in the same fiscal year. Therefore, to clearly reflect the business's income, the income and expenses should be allocated to their respective periods. It is important to note that only small contractors and any home construction contracts may use the completed contract method.

Look-back method for percentage of completion. According to Reg. 1.460-6, the look-back method is a calculation of additional interest that needs to be paid to (or refunded by) the IRS on taxes paid on contract revenue that has been recognized in prior years using the percentage of completion method. The tax code requires those using the percentage of completion method to recompute the prior year's taxes based on actual costs if the contractor estimates of costs were incorrect. A contractor may elect out of the look-back rule if the tax using estimated cost is within 10% of the tax using the actual costs. This rule does not apply to small contractors whose average annual gross receipts for the three years do not exceed $10 million or for contracts that are expected to be completed within two years. Valuation analysts should be careful to review a construction company's financials when the company uses the percentage of completion method as they will need to consider the look-back method in their valuation.

Homebuilders. For income tax purposes, homebuilders treat their speculative homes (spec homes) as inventory. Homebuilders are also subject to the uniform capitalization rules under IRC § 263A, which outline whether a cost must be capitalized versus expensed. However, "small" contractors are exempt. Homebuilders are prevented from using the percentage of completion method under the tax code.

New tax rates. One of the more important provisions in P.L. 115-97, known as the Tax Cuts and Jobs Act, enacted Dec. 22, 2017, is the new Sec. 199A—the deduction for qualified business income (QBI). Sec. 199A allows a deduction for up to 20% of QBI from partnerships, limited liability companies (LLCs), S corporations, trusts, estates, and sole proprietorships. Sec. 199A creates a deduction based on an artificial calculation of business income instead of actual economic outlays required for most other business deductions. The provision is a significant tax benefit for many noncorporate businesses and was passed as a result of the tax rates declining from a maximum graduated rate of 35% down to a flat 21% rate. The Sec. 199A deduction is taken at the partner, S corporation shareholder, estate and trust, or sole proprietor level for tax years beginning after Dec. 31, 2017, and goes through tax years ending Dec. 31, 2025. This is a critical thing that the valuation analysist needs to consider when determining the appropriate tax rate to apply to the projections and future income.

Common asset types for construction companies. The final section of this chapter addresses the common type of assets that construction companies have.

Equipment. The types of equipment construction contractors hold can vary widely. The heavy construction trades, such as excavating, highway construction, and bridge building, require significant capital investment in heavy equipment, such as earth-moving equipment, cranes, concrete pumpers, and so on, which are expensive to purchase and maintain.

Many general contractors can operate with minimal amounts of heavy equipment. More common types of equipment, such as backhoes, may be rented, thus avoiding large capital expenditures.

Goodwill. Because of intense price competition in the industry, many construction contractors have little, if any, goodwill value. This stems from the low margins that result from the competitive bidding process. Contractors who have goodwill tend to have more negotiated contracts than competitively bid contracts and may have a good reputation and/or good relationship with customers.

Nonoperating assets. Construction contractors frequently maintain levels of working capital and debt capacity that would be considered in excess of operating needs in other industries. Excess working capital and excess debt capacity enhance the amount of bonding credit a contractor can secure. The more bonding credit that a contractor can secure, the more the contractor can grow its business. Accordingly, working capital and debt capacity need to be evaluated in light of a construction contractor's bonding credit needs.

3. Methods for Valuing Construction Companies

By Pasquale Rafanelli

There are many factors to consider in the valuation of a closely held company. Many of these factors are described in Internal Revenue Service Revenue Ruling 59-60. We consider the guidelines set forth in this revenue ruling and the factors described therein when preparing valuations. As such, the valuation process considers the facts and circumstances of the business valuator's analysis to determine which approaches and their underlying methods to apply in a particular engagement.

Approaches to valuation. There are three traditional approaches to valuing a closely held business such as a privately owned construction company: the asset approach, the market approach, and the income approach.

The asset approach. This approach considers the tangible net asset value of the assets and liabilities of the enterprise under conditions of an orderly liquidation. The normal procedure is to adjust each item on the subject company's balance sheet to reflect the cash result of an orderly liquidation. Transaction costs are factored into the value and thus calculated.

The competitive bidding environment inherent in construction companies drives profit margins down to the point that values are frequently near net asset value. Contracting companies, particularly those that are smaller, are often sold at or near book value because barriers to entry are minimal, causing many to start their own business rather than purchase an existing contractor.

The market approach. This approach is a process of comparing prices paid in transactions for comparable businesses that have a satisfactory degree of similarity to the subject enterprise. The market approach is based on the principle of substitution, which implies that the market value is equal to the cost to buy a comparable substitute. Comparable transactions can be stock exchange transactions of public companies or the sales of a small private business in a negotiated transaction.

Most publicly traded construction companies are diversified, offering engineering and other products and services. Most of the publicly traded homebuilders also offer mortgage services. Lists of publicly traded construction companies can be found on several websites, including Yahoo! Finance's Industry Center, PitchBook, Capital IQ, and more.

Databases of private-company transactions include data on acquisitions of construction contractors, but they can cause challenges in deriving a value because of the limited information available on each deal. Furthermore, the valuation analyst often cannot determine the comparability of the transactions because the motivations of the buyer and the seller are unknown or the information in the databases may not have been reported correctly. Nevertheless, business valuators utilize these data sources because, when properly used and understood, they generally provide good information on actual sales of small private companies—data that are difficult to find. Some of the more common private transaction databases include but are not limited to DealStats, BIZCOMPS, and ValuSource Market Comps (IBA).

The income approach. This approach is the capitalization of anticipated earnings at an appropriate capitalization rate with respect to the anticipated risk of the enterprise. The income approach is based on the premise that a prudent investor would pay no more for an investment than he or she would for an alternative investment with similar characteristics of risk and return. There are two primary methods under the income approach:

- Capitalization of earnings method; and
- Discounted cash flows method.

Both methods discount a projected future income stream to the present value. The capitalization of cash flow method requires the projection of only one future period, whereas the discounted cash flow (DCF) method requires an income projection for two periods or more into the future.

The DCF method is a "two-stage model that projects economic income for a finite number of periods, usually one business cycle of somewhere between three and 10 years, and then assumes a terminal value at the end of the discrete projection period."[1]

There are three preconditions for which, if they are met, the capitalization of cash flows method is preferred because it is more simple to apply. These preconditions are:

- The first projected period has a level of economic benefits that is representative of future economic benefits;
- The future economic benefits are expected to increase at a constant rate of growth; and
- The future economic benefits will be realized for a relatively long period.

An advantage to using the DCF method with construction contractors who use the percentage of completion accounting method is that cash flow forecasts and management's accuracy in estimating project costs can be checked by:

- Comparing the individual completed projects prior-period job schedules to determine how accurate the estimating has been historically; and
- Analyzing backlog (both projects in process and projects not yet started) to determine viability of forecasts.

The capitalization of cash flow method assumes that margins and growth will remain constant into the future. A contractor's level of backlog can help the valuation professional support or dispute the constant growth assumption of the capitalized cash flow method.

Risks in the construction industry. There are many inherent risks in the construction industry—all of which have a direct impact on the risk associated with the business and ultimately the value. Some of the major risks are covered as follows.

The business cycle. The construction industry fluctuates between highs and lows, typically over periods of between five and 10 years. It is extremely sensitive to changes in both the

1 S.P. Pratt and A.V. Niculita, *Valuing a Business: The Analysis and Appraisal of Closely Held Companies*, New York: McGraw-Hill, pg. 186, emphasis in the original.

overall economy as well as fluctuations in interest rates. Also, the cycle is often different for commercial, residential, and infrastructure construction and varies based upon the company's level of specialization and whether it is operating in the private or public sector.

Management and leadership. In the construction industry, most jobs are contracted based upon a highly competitive bidding process. The company's ability to continue developing bids that are both attractive to the customer and profitable to the company is paramount in determining future earnings capacity. Furthermore, the company may be dependent on key relationships with suppliers or vendors in generating its current bids. If the company relies on one individual or a small group of key people who have all of the expertise and maintain all of the relationships, a significant business risk must be taken into consideration when valuing the company.

Cyclicality. The construction industry is cyclical. Demand for construction services is highly dependent on the health of the economy and is affected by outside forces such as interest rates, governmental spending, and corporate growth.

Losses from projects. Construction contractors can experience losses from issues out of their control, such as weather delays, a subcontractor's poor workmanship, or unforeseen difficulties during the construction process. Profit margins are so thin that losses from a single job can cause an entire construction company to be unprofitable and can even lead to bankruptcy.

Personnel. Many construction contractors heavily rely on highly skilled craftspeople such as estimators, heavy-equipment operators, plumbers, and electricians. A contractor's profitability and work quality relate directly to such employees. Contractors also use unskilled workers. The use of undocumented immigrants may be an area of potential liability for contractors. Contractors who hire undocumented immigrants, whether unwittingly or knowingly, risk fines and other penalties.

Employee safety. The construction industry has the largest share of fatalities of any industry. Contractors can face significant liability in the event of the injury or death of an employee.

Insurance costs. The inherent risks in the construction industry cause contractors to pay higher premiums for all types of insurance. The areas that cause most concern are construction defects, inexperienced employees, and poor bookkeeping.

Supplies and materials. Materials used in construction are either commodities or near commodities, such as lumber products, steel, concrete, wallboard, etc. Fuel prices tend to have a significant impact on construction contractors, especially those who operate heavy equipment. Fluctuations in commodity prices can make estimating costs difficult and will ultimately impact profitability.

Operational and industrial issues. Similar to the risks involved in the construction industry, there are operational and industrial issues to take into consideration when valuing a company in this industry.

Estimating. Estimators compute the contractor's cost of completing a project. If the estimates are too high, the contractor can potentially outbid the contract and not secure the project. If the estimates are too low, it could lead to financial losses, which could have a long-lasting impact on the company's future success. Accuracy in estimating is vital to the success of a contractor, and a good estimating staff can be invaluable.

Some of the common errors in construction cost estimating are:

- Arithmetic errors;
- Incorrect measurement (e.g., project size, materials requirements, labor hours, etc.);
- Incorrect labor rates;
- Incorrect pricing of materials;
- Not performing a site visit;
- Overlooking haulage costs;
- Failure to review building codes;
- Omitting items considered to be minor;
- Failure to carefully review bids of subcontractors; and
- Inadequate consideration of overhead charges.

Financing capacity. Many contracts require construction companies to be bonded to provide the project owner assurance that the job will proceed as scheduled. To obtain a bond, the company is often required to meet strict financial covenants. It is important to understand whether the company is generally subject to bonding, such as is required in the public sector, and to analyze whether the company can continue to meet the financial covenants to obtain the bonds. When preparing a valuation, a key component is to do a thorough financial analysis. For a construction company, this is critical not only for the historical performance, but also for future performance. The primary driver of the concluded value in construction companies is typically future earnings, which are based on projections. If the projections do not meet and cannot support the requirements, then the value is meaningless as it cannot be achieved.

Bonding. A surety bond is a guarantee to the owner of a project on the performance of the contractor. Project owners typically require contractors to have a surety bond to protect themselves. Typically, each project has its own surety bond associated with it.

The three types of surety bonds are:

- *Bid bond.* Provides a financial guarantee that the bid has been submitted in good faith and that the bidder intends to enter into the contract at the bid price. This prevents the construction company from being the lowest bidder and unilaterally deciding to walk away. If the construction company was to walk away, it would forfeit the bond.

- *Performance bond.* Protects the project owner from financial losses if the contractor should fail to perform under the contract. This prevents the contractor from walking away midproject or not performing the project in accordance with the contract.

- *Payment bond.* Guarantees that the contractor will pay subcontractors. This prevents the contractor from not paying its subcontractors (i.e., electricians, plumbers, etc.) for specialized work performed in accordance with their contract.

Based on discussions with bonding agents, the amount of bonding credit extended is typically a multiple of working capital and/or net worth. This multiple typically ranges between five and 20 times, and the premium on the surety bond is approximately 1.0% to 1.5% of the total contract revenue. The amount of the surety bonding credit to extend is based heavily on a contractor's financial statements. As a result, contractors are often required to provide reviewed or audited financial statements.

The surety generally looks upon overbillings favorably, even though they are a liability. Overbillings indicate that the contractor is aggressive in his or her billing policies and that the project owner, not the contractor, is financing the project. However, excessive overbilling is not looked on favorably because job borrowing (when overbillings exceed the estimated gross profit on the project) is viewed unfavorably.

A reduction in the amount of bonding credit can have a devastating financial effect on a contractor. To maximize the amount of bonding credit, contractors tend to have high current ratios and low levels of debt.

To determine working capital and net worth, surety agents will typically prepare a balance sheet assessment similar to the exhibit.

Sample Balance Sheet Assessment		
Balance Sheet Item	**Included in Working Capital**	**Included in Net Worth**
Cash	Included in Full	Allowed in Full
Marketable Securities	Included in Full	Allowed in Full
A/R	Under 90 Days Included	Over 90 Days Considered
Retention	Included	Allowed
Underbillings	Included	Included
Inventory	Included 50% to 80%	Allowed 50% to 80%
Prepaid Expenses	Not Included	Allowed
Cash Value of Life Insurance	Included	Allowed
Fixed Assets	Not Included	Allowed per Books
Shareholder Receivable	Not Included	Not Allowed
Goodwill	Not Included	Not Allowed
Intangible Assets	Not Included	Not Allowed
Liabilities	Generally as Booked	Generally as Booked
Overbillings	Included	Included

Competitive bidding. Most contractors secure work through a competitive bidding process. A project owner invites contractors to bid on a project and then awards it to the contractor with the best bid. In some cases, the lowest bid is not always the best bid, but the amount of the bid is always a critical factor. As a result, this process can potentially be a double-edged sword for the contractor. Bids must be low enough to be attractive to the project owner but high enough to complete a project in a profitable fashion.

Backlog of work. Unless the economy changes or management indicates otherwise, the valuator can typically use historical operations to project the company's future earnings capacity. This is done using the logic that the customers will stay with the company and the business cycle will continue. The projection of future earnings can tend to be more difficult in the construction industry because, although the company has customers and contracts today, it cannot be assumed or guaranteed that those earnings will remain steady or even continue to grow into the future. The sustainability of construction revenues is highly dependent on the continuing availability of the specific contractor's work. In the construction industry, the backlog, which is also known as "work not yet completed," is a much better indicator of what earnings the company expects in the future. It would be grossly inaccurate for the valuator to ignore the backlog when valuing a construction company. Remember the housing crisis of 2008, which led to the downturn in the economy? That crisis caused several construction companies to struggle and many to even close their doors. Unlike the retail industry, which, in most cases, is a necessity, residential or commercial construction is often a cosmetic desire rather than a need. Therefore, a down economy can really hurt the construction industry.

Equipment. Typically, one of the most important assets a construction company has is its equipment, which is either purchased or leased. Often, the equipment's fair market value can be significantly different than book value, and, in some cases, it can actually be higher. As a result, like real estate, the valuation analyst could be required to hire a qualified equipment appraisal to determine the fair market value of the specialized equipment. Moreover, leases should be analyzed to determine remaining lives and the potential for increased costs as replacements become necessary.

Litigation risk. The construction industry is highly litigious. Contractual disputes and workplace accidents can subject the company to significant litigation-related costs.

Regulatory risk. The construction industry is highly dependent on regulatory issues. Contractors need to ensure that they are compliant with federal, state, and local laws. It is the contractor's responsibility to ensure he or she fully understands all the laws and regulations and that the company and its employees are fully compliant with these regulations.

Weather. Weather plays a big role in the construction industry, especially if the work is performed outside. There can be ample delays and/or damage that require work to be reproduced and additional expenses to be incurred. These delays could cause massive fines and loss of performance bonding if key milestones are not met. This could also cause the company to pay additional money in overtime and bring in additional support, which may not be reimbursed by the project owner and cause less income or even incur a loss for the company.

Valuation nuances. Valuation analysts should pay particular attention to the following nuances encountered in the construction industry.

Underbillings and overbillings. Underbillings and overbillings are included in working capital for valuation purposes. If an analyst uses historical cash flows to arrive at a value for a construction company, then the cash flows already incorporate adjustments for job profitability. These adjustments include modifications to the amount of revenue recognized, underbillings, and overbillings. If the company uses the look-back method for tax purposes and the underbillings or overbillings were estimated incorrectly, an adjustment would be required to properly state the assets or liability. The offset accounting would be revenue, and, as a result, the cash flow would not change. Therefore, change in revenue and the changes in the underbillings and overbillings would offset and the resulting cash flows would remain the same under either method.

Assets and debt capacity. Assets and debt capacity that initially appear to be in excess of needs may actually be required to maintain bonding credit amounts. Therefore, a typical adjustment to make under ordinary circumstance may be inappropriate when valuing a construction company.

Estimated growth rates. Estimated future growth rates may be constrained by bonding credit levels and the company's ability to increase those levels. Therefore, future growth rates used should be supportable and achievable based on the actual levels of the company.

Rules of thumb. Rules of thumb are provided as a broad benchmark to assess reasonableness of a valuation conclusion. The facts and circumstances of each individual company should be considered in determining the value of that particular company. General rules of thumb for construction valuations include:

- Book value;
- Book value plus a multiple of backlog;
- Ten percent to 30% of annual revenues; and
- Two to 3.5 times cash flows.

The value of a general contractor's business tends to be on the lower end of the spectrum, while the value of specialty contractors tends to be on the higher end of the spectrum.

Conclusion. Conclusions of value for a construction company will vary based on the region, name recognition, financial strength, and other factors as discussed throughout this chapter and determined when performing the valuation.

4. Case Study: A Walk Through the Valuation of a Residential/Commercial Construction Company

By Pasquale Rafanelli

This chapter presents a case study of a construction company for the purposes of outlining several of the factors that go into the valuation of a privately held business. This case study is meant for demonstration purposes only.

Company Overview

Potter LLC (Potter) is a Long Island-based limited liability company that was formed on Jan. 1, 1980. Potter is located at 1234 James Ave., Merrick, N.Y. The company provides construction services to both the residential sector and commercial sector. Based on discussion with management and a review of their jobs over the last five years, the revenues are equally split between the residential projects and the commercial projects.

The company has a total of 50 employees. The following individuals are involved in the management of the business:

- Katerina Potter, director/CEO;
- Damon Potter, CFO; and
- Arya Potter, COO.

Damon Potter and Katerina Potter are husband and wife. Arya Potter is their daughter.

Ownership

The ownership structure as of Dec. 31, 2017, is as follows:

Owner Name	% Owned	Title
Katerina Potter	50%	Director/CEO
Damon Potter	50%	CFO

The purpose of the valuation is for Katerina Potter and Damon Potter to each gift a 1% interest to their three children: Arya Potter, Frances Potter, and Frank Potter.

Competition

The company operates in the residential and commercial construction industry, which both large and small companies dominate in a highly concentrated manner.

Prior Transactions in the Company's Securities

There have been no transactions in the company's securities since its inception.

Financial Analysis

Adjustments

A key step in the valuation process is to analyze the historical financial data for nonrecurring or discretionary items. In this case, valuation is a forward-looking concept. Consequently, an estimate of future prospects, not the past operating results, is necessary to approximate income without the presence of nonrecurring or discretionary items. The purpose of the following adjustments is to determine the potential future operating results that a hypothetical buyer of a minority interest may expect. Therefore, we have prepared various schedules to detail valuation adjustments, if any. The following adjustments were made to the company's balance sheets and income statements and can be found in the exhibits throughout this chapter. Below is a discussion of the adjusted financial information.

Balance Sheets

The following is a discussion of the adjustments to the balance sheets for the purposes of valuation.

1. *Shareholder loans.* The loans from the shareholders are presented on the balance sheet as liabilities (see Exhibit 1). Based on discussions with management, Katerina Potter and

Damon Potter made the loans equally in 2013, and they have remained on the balance sheet since. The amounts have not been repaid, and, according to management, there is no intention for the company to pay them back. Therefore, we have reclassified it to equity as a capital contribution the owners made.

Exhibit 1. Loan From Shareholders

	2012	2013	2014	2015	2016	2017
Shareholder loan	-	(2,000,000)	(2,000,000)	(2,000,000)	(2,000,000)	(2,000,000)

2. *Cost in excess of billings.* We performed a thorough analysis of the company's current open projects, looking specifically at the proposals, contracts, budgets, and works in progress (WIP) schedules. We then interviewed management and key project managers to ascertain the current status of the jobs and the percentage of completion. Based on this analysis, we have determined that the cost in excess of billings is appropriately stated and reflects the current value. Therefore, we have not made any adjustments to the balance sheet.

3. *Billings in excess of costs.* We performed a thorough analysis of the current open projects looking specifically at the proposals, contracts, budgets, and WIP schedules. We then interviewed management and key project managers to ascertain the current status of the jobs and the percentage of completion. Based on this analysis, we have determined that the billings in excess of costs are appropriately stated and reflect the current value. Therefore, we have not made any adjustments to the balance.

Income Statements

The following is a discussion of the adjustments to the income statements.

1. *Salaries expense.* Based on discussions with management, all wages and payroll taxes for both direct employees (all employees on job sites) and indirect employees (office staff) are reported as a single amount in the cost of goods sold (COGS) section of the balance sheet. Therefore, we have removed the portion of the wages and payroll taxes that are associated with indirect employees and have moved it to the operating expenses section (see Exhibit 2). This adjustment was made to avoid distorting the business's gross profit and operating income and to properly reflect the income statement. There is no impact on the net income as it is a reclassifying adjustment.

Exhibit 2. Salaries Expense						
	2012 ($)	2013 ($)	2014 ($)	2015 ($)	2016 ($)	2017 ($)
Wages—COGS	(63,917)	(57,446)	(183,267)	(349,113)	(334,007)	(410,444)
Salaries—operating	59,046	53,068	169,300	322,506	308,551	379,163
Payroll taxes—operating	4,871	4,378	13,967	26,607	25,455	31,281
Owners' compensation—as reported	(84,638)	(25,899)	(110,047)	(198,199)	(202,046)	(183,922)
Normalized owners' compensation (see Exhibit 4)	486,000	489,900	654,700	783,700	798,900	863,500

2. *Miscellaneous expense.* Based on discussions with management, the miscellaneous expenses are not business-related expenses and are actually the owners' personal and discretionary items that the business pays for (see Exhibit 3). Therefore, we have added the miscellaneous expense back as a nonbusiness and discretionary expense.

Exhibit 3. Miscellaneous Expenses						
	2012 ($)	2013 ($)	2014 ($)	2015 ($)	2016 ($)	2017 ($)
Miscellaneous—COGS	(173,083)	(462,381)	(1,155,281)	(2,990,936)	(3,632,881)	(3,311,909)

3. *Owners' compensation.* We have researched the ERI[1] database for the compensation benchmarks for a president and a vice president in the residential and commercial construction industry in the New York state region, with revenues equal to the company's revenues each year from 2012 to 2017 and have arrived at estimated salaries shown in Exhibit 4.

Exhibit 4. Estimated Owners' Salaries						
	2012 ($)	2013 ($)	2014 ($)	2015 ($)	2016 ($)	2017 ($)
President	305,100	306,700	429,800	522,300	532,800	578,800
Vice president	180,900	183,200	224,900	261,400	266,100	284,700
Total	**486,000**	**489,900**	**654,700**	**783,700**	**798,900**	**863,500**

We have, therefore, adjusted owners' compensation to the amounts shown in Exhibit 4 to reflect a reasonable salary.

4. *Tax affecting adjustment for pass-through entities.* The company is set up as an S corporation, and, in this structure, distributions are made to the shareholders who are then responsible for the tax (i.e., the company is not taxed). We have tax affected the

1 ERI Economic Research Institute, Redmond, Wash., erieri.com.

company using an appropriate tax rate as calculated in the Delaware Chancery model (see Exhibit 5).

Exhibit 5. Delaware Chancery Model for Historical Periods			
	C Corp.	S Corp.	S Corp. Valuation
Income before tax	$100.00	$100.00	$100.00
Corporate tax rate	40.70%	0.00%	26.67%
Available earnings	$59.30	$100.00	$73.33
Dividend or personal income tax rate (federal and state)	29.13%	44.93%	29.13%
Differential between corporate and personal rates			-4.23%
Available after dividends	$42.03	$55.07	$55.07

It is important to note the tax rate of 26.67% listed in Exhibit 5 for a pass-through entity to be used in the years prior to 2018 is based on the Delaware Chancery model for a company that is located on Long Island, N.Y. It includes the appropriate rate and tax effective rates for the federal, state, and MTA surcharge. Every state and jurisdiction would need to compute the tax rate for a pass-through entity using the appropriate and applicable tax and effective tax rates.

Adjusted Statements

As part of this valuation, we prepared various schedules detailing the past financial results and incorporated any adjustments that were made (as discussed in the "Adjustments" section of this chapter) to develop adjusted financial statements. The following is a discussion of the adjusted financial information.

Balance Sheets

Significant items and trends concerning the company after the adjustments were made include:

1. The company's cash represents its largest asset, and it is separated into two distinct classes: cash and restricted cash. The restricted cash is the cash that the company is required to keep on hand at all times for bonding purposes. The cash account has fluctuated during the period, ranging from a high of approximately 82.2% of total assets as of Dec. 31, 2013, to a low of approximately 18.1% of total assets as of Dec. 31, 2017 (see Exhibit 6).

Exhibit 6. Cash Trend											
2012		2013		2014		2015		2016		2017	
$3,914,616.0	62.6%	$9,906,887.0	82.2%	$16,441,395.0	73.9%	$15,214,847.0	52.2%	$7,860,644.0	25.6%	$6,173,414.0	18.1%

2. The restricted cash account has increased since 2014, ranging from a low of approximately 6.8% of total assets as of Dec. 31, 2014, to a high of approximately 52.1% of total assets as of Dec. 31, 2017 (see Exhibit 7).

Exhibit 7. Restricted Cash Trend											
2012		2013		2014		2015		2016		2017	
-	0.0%	-	0.0%	$1,502,089	6.8%	$4,659,080	16.0%	$11,186,496	36.4%	$17,743,110	52.1%

3. The company's property, plant and equipment (PPE) net has fluctuated, ranging from a low of approximately 0.4% of total assets as of Dec. 31, 2014, to a high of about 4.2% of total assets as of Dec. 31, 2015, and Dec. 31, 2016 (see Exhibit 8).

Exhibit 8. Property Plant and Equipment Trend											
2012		2013		2014		2015		2016		2017	
$118,913	1.9%	$99,854	0.8%	$80,798	0.4%	$1,219,152	4.2%	$1,277,291	4.2%	$1,288,523	3.8%

4. Total assets have increased from a low of approximately $6.2 million as of Dec. 31, 2012, to a high of about $34.1 million as of Dec. 31, 2017 (Exhibit 9).

Exhibit 9. Total Asset Trend											
2012		2013		2014		2015		2016		2017	
$6,249,959	100.0%	$12,058,923	100.0%	$22,243,515	100.0%	$29,120,479	100.0%	$30,756,839	100.0%	$34,065,018	100.0%

5. The company's accounts payable represents its largest liability, which ranges from a low of approximately 8.5% of total assets as of Dec. 31, 2013, to a high of about 22.6% of total assets as of Dec. 31, 2017 (see Exhibit 10).

Exhibit 10. Accounts Payable Trend											
2012		2013		2014		2015		2016		2017	
$1,136,911	18.2%	$1,030,544	8.5%	$3,255,688	14.6%	$6,481,030	22.3%	$6,264,463	20.4%	$7,686,060	22.6%

6. Total liabilities have increased from a low of approximately $3.6 million as of Dec. 31, 2012, to a high of approximately $28.7 million (84.3% of total assets) as of Dec. 31, 2017 (see Exhibit 11).

Exhibit 11. Total Liabilities Trend											
2012		2013		2014		2015		2016		2017	
$3,637,185	58.2%	$7,424,484	61.6%	$17,522,682	78.8%	$24,230,016	83.2%	$25,673,789	83.5%	$28,722,107	84.3%

7. The company's equity has increased from a low of approximately $2.6 million as of Dec. 31, 2012, to a high of approximately $5.3 million (15.7% of total assets) as of Dec. 31, 2017 (see Exhibit 12).

Exhibit 12. Total Equity Trend											
2012		2013		2014		2015		2016		2017	
$2,612,774	41.8%	$4,634,439	38.4%	$4,720,833	21.2%	$4,890,463	16.8%	$5,083,050	16.5%	$5,342,911	15.7%

Overall, the company compares unfavorably to its peers in that its current asset balance is slightly above its peers, its total debt is above its peers, and it has an equity balance that is below that of its peers.

Income Statements

The significant items and trends concerning the company after we made income statement adjustments include:

1. The company's net revenues have fluctuated, from a low of about $5.3 million in 2013 to a high of approximately $37.9 million in 2017, with a compounded annual growth rate (CAGR) from 2012 to 2017 of approximately 45.1% of revenues (see Exhibit 13).

Exhibit 13. Revenue Trend											
2012		2013		2014		2015		2016		2017	
$5,904,585	100.0%	$5,306,798	100.0%	$16,929,961	100.0%	$32,250,599	100.0%	$30,855,134	100.0%	$37,916,337	100.0%

2. The company's gross profit as a percentage of sales has fluctuated, from a low of approximately 8.9% of revenues in 2012 to a high of about 17.2% of revenues in 2016. For the year ended Dec. 31, 2017, the gross profit was approximately 13.6% of revenues (See Exhibit 14).

Exhibit 14. Gross Profit Trend											
2012		2013		2014		2015		2016		2017	
$526,051	8.9%	$682,791	12.9%	$2,013,986	11.9%	$4,597,241	14.3%	$5,298,733	17.2%	$5,139,600	13.6%

3. Operating expenses as a percentage of revenues have decreased from a high of about 2.0% of revenues in 2012 to a low of approximately 1.2% of revenues from 2015 through 2017 (see Exhibit 15).

Exhibit 15. Operating Expenses Trend											
2012		2013		2014		2015		2016		2017	
$118,921	2.0%	$76,973	1.5%	$211,686	1.3%	$396,943	1.2%	$379,990	1.2%	$472,959	1.2%

4. EBITDA has increased from a low of about -$78,900, or approximately -1.3% of revenues, in 2012 to a high of approximately $4.1 million, or 13.4%, in 2016. EBITDA was approximately $3.8 million, or 10.0%, for the year ended Dec. 31, 2017 (see Exhibit 16).

Exhibit 16. EBITDA Trend											
2012		2013		2014		2015		2016		2017	
$(78,870)	-1.3%	$115,918	2.2%	$1,147,600	6.8%	$3,416,598	10.6%	$4,119,843	13.4%	$3,803,141	10.0%

5. EBIT has increased from a low of -$105,290, or about -1.8% of revenues, in 2012 to a high of about $4.1 million, or 13.2%, in 2016. EBIT was approximately $3.7 million, or about 9.9%, for the year ended Dec. 31, 2017 (see Exhibit 17).

Exhibit 17. EBIT Trend											
2012		2013		2014		2015		2016		2017	
$(105,290)	-1.8%	$113,584	2.1%	$1,141,403	6.7%	$3,399,664	10.5%	$4,078,417	13.2%	$3,747,100	9.9%

6. Pretax income has increased from a low of approximately -$107,000, or about -1.8% of revenues, in 2012 to a high of almost $4.0 million, or 12.9%, in 2016. Pretax income was about $3.6 million, or 9.6%, for the year ended Dec. 31, 2017 (see Exhibit 18).

Exhibit 18. Pretax Income/(Loss) Trend											
2012		2013		2014		2015		2016		2017	
$(106,998)	-1.8%	$83,084	1.6%	$1,068,203	6.3%	$3,320,361	10.3%	$3,968,877	12.9%	$3,637,397	9.6%

The following are the significant items and trends that occurred during the period analyzed (2012 through 2017):

1. Revenues increased during the period analyzed;
2. Gross margins fluctuated during the period analyzed; and
3. EBITDA, EBIT, and pretax income all increased during the period analyzed (2012 through 2016) and decreased in 2017.

Overall, the company does well, as it is outperforming its peers in gross profit and pretax income, which are important metrics for investors.

Financial Ratio Analysis[2]

An analysis of the financial and operating ratios for the company provides further insight into its operating results and efficiencies. Analysis of financial statement ratios can help highlight some of a company's strengths and weaknesses. These strengths and weaknesses can be observed over time as the company's operations change and can also be measured relative to other businesses in the same industry.

In addition to reviewing the company's financial statements, it is also critical to compare the company's financial position and results of operations to that of its peers in its industry. This analysis is important because the trends and ratios need to be put into a broader context to make valid interpretations and conclusions regarding the company's financial position, operating results, and future earnings potential.

See Exhibit 19 for a comparison of the company's financial metrics to those of its peers.

Exhibit 19. Residential and Commercial Builder Financial Metric Comparisons

		2013	2014	2015	2016	2017
Gross margin	Company	12.9%	11.9%	14.3%	17.2%	13.6%
	Industry	11.5%	10.3%	10.9%	11.9%	11.5%
	Performance	Outperforming	Outperforming	Outperforming	Outperforming	Outperforming
		2013	2014	2015	2016	2017
Sales to net worth	Company	1.15	3.59	6.59	6.07	7.10
	Industry	7.84	8.99	9.52	9.27	10.50
	Performance	Underperforming	Underperforming	Underperforming	Underperforming	Underperforming
		2013	2014	2015	2016	2017
Pretax return on revenues	Company	1.6%	6.3%	10.3%	12.9%	9.6%
	Industry	3.1%	2.7%	3.1%	3.5%	3.9%
	Performance	Underperforming	Outperforming	Outperforming	Outperforming	Outperforming
		2013	2014	2015	2016	2017
Pretax return on assets	Company	0.7%	4.8%	11.4%	12.9%	10.7%
	Industry	7.8%	7.2%	8.2%	9.4%	10.9%
	Performance	Underperforming	Underperforming	Outperforming	Outperforming	Neutral
		2013	2014	2015	2016	2017
Pretax return on equity	Company	1.8%	22.6%	67.9%	78.1%	68.1%
	Industry	24.6%	24.4%	29.3%	32.7%	40.4%
	Performance	Underperforming	Neutral	Outperforming	Outperforming	Outperforming

Exhibit 19 continued on next page.

2 Unless otherwise stated, data for the industry are medians and data for the company are averages.

Exhibit 19. Residential and Commercial Builder Financial Metric Comparisons

		2013	2014	2015	2016	2017
Depreciation, and amortization to sales	Company	0.0%	0.0%	0.1%	0.1%	0.1%
	Industry	0.3%	0.2%	0.2%	0.3%	0.2%
	Performance	Outperforming	Outperforming	Outperforming	Outperforming	Outperforming
		2013	2014	2015	2016	2017
Officer's compensation	Company	9.2%	3.9%	2.4%	2.6%	2.3%
	Industry	n/a	0.8%	0.9%	1.0%	n/a
	Performance	n/a	Outperforming	Outperforming	Outperforming	n/a
		2013	2014	2015	2016	2017
Total debt to total assets	Company	0.62	0.79	0.83	0.83	0.84
	Industry	0.68	0.71	0.72	0.71	0.73
	Performance	Neutral	Underperforming	Underperforming	Underperforming	Underperforming
		2013	2014	2015	2016	2017
Total debt to equity	Company	1.60	3.71	4.95	5.05	5.38
	Industry	2.17	2.40	2.56	2.49	2.72
	Performance	Outperforming	Underperforming	Underperforming	Underperforming	Underperforming
		2013	2014	2015	2016	2017
Long-term debt to total assets	Company	0.00	0.00	0.03	0.03	0.02
	Industry	0.07	0.07	0.07	0.08	0.08
	Performance	Outperforming	Outperforming	Outperforming	Outperforming	Outperforming
		2013	2014	2015	2016	2017
Times interest earned	Company	3.72	15.59	42.87	37.23	34.16
	Industry	18.35	21.73	24.25	23.28	28.88
	Performance	Underperforming	Underperforming	Outperforming	Outperforming	Outperforming
		2013	2014	2015	2016	2017
Current ratio	Company	1.62	1.27	1.19	1.18	1.17
	Industry	1.35	1.30	1.28	1.35	1.28
	Performance	Outperforming	Neutral	Neutral	Underperforming	Neutral
		2013	2014	2015	2016	2017
Quick ratio	Company	1.62	1.27	1.19	1.18	1.17
	Industry	0.95	0.88	0.88	0.88	0.88
	Performance	Outperforming	Outperforming	Outperforming	Outperforming	Outperforming
		2013	2014	2015	2016	2017
Accounts receivable to revenues	Company	21.1%	13.1%	15.2%	20.5%	18.1%
	Industry	16.0%	13.6%	14.3%	14.6%	13.9%
	Performance	Underperforming	Neutral	Neutral	Underperforming	Underperforming
		2013	2014	2015	2016	2017
Working capital to sales	Company	67.2%	27.2%	14.2%	14.8%	12.4%
	Industry	8.8%	7.7%	7.3%	7.9%	7.1%
	Performance	Outperforming	Outperforming	Outperforming	Outperforming	Outperforming

Exhibit 19 continued on next page.

Exhibit 19. Residential and Commercial Builder Financial Metric Comparisons (continued)						
		2013	2014	2015	2016	2017
Working capital	Company	4,571,314	4,654,065	4,503,912	4,601,092	4,823,321
	Industry	8,693,700	8,485,700	8,341,200	9,236,300	8,646,300
	Performance	Underperforming	Underperforming	Underperforming	Underperforming	Underperforming
		2013	2014	2015	2016	2017
Cash turnover	Company	0.77	1.29	2.04	2.67	5.40
	Industry	9.90	11.90	12.00	12.90	13.40
	Performance	Underperforming	Underperforming	Underperforming	Underperforming	Underperforming
		2013	2014	2015	2016	2017
Accounts receivable turnover	Company	4.73	7.61	6.56	4.89	5.51
	Industry	6.29	7.30	7.02	6.89	7.16
	Performance	Underperforming	Neutral	Neutral	Underperforming	Underperforming
		2013	2014	2015	2016	2017
Receivable collection period, days	Company	77	48	56	75	66
	Industry	58	50	52	53	51
	Performance	Underperforming	Neutral	Neutral	Underperforming	Underperforming
		2013	2014	2015	2016	2017
Accounts payable turnover	Company	4.27	6.96	5.68	4.01	4.70
	Industry	6.29	7.30	6.76	6.76	7.16
	Performance	Underperforming	Neutral	Underperforming	Underperforming	Underperforming
		2013	2014	2015	2016	2017
Days accounts payable	Company	86	52	64	91	78
	Industry	58	50	54	54	51
	Performance	Underperforming	Neutral	Underperforming	Underperforming	Underperforming
		2013	2014	2015	2016	2017
Asset turnover	Company	0.58	0.99	1.26	1.03	1.17
	Industry	2.30	2.70	2.70	2.70	2.80
	Performance	Underperforming	Underperforming	Underperforming	Underperforming	Underperforming
		2013	2014	2015	2016	2017
Current asset turnover	Company	0.59	0.99	1.29	1.08	1.22
	Industry	2.80	3.20	3.20	3.20	3.30
	Performance	Underperforming	Underperforming	Underperforming	Underperforming	Underperforming
		2013	2014	2015	2016	2017
Working capital turnover	Company	1.49	3.67	7.04	6.78	8.05
	Industry	10.78	12.91	13.55	13.38	13.66
	Performance	Underperforming	Underperforming	Underperforming	Underperforming	Underperforming
		2013	2014	2015	2016	2017
Fixed asset turnover	Company	48.52	187.43	49.62	24.72	29.56
	Industry	27.03	36.09	36.19	35.76	36.38
	Performance	Outperforming	Outperforming	Outperforming	Underperforming	Underperforming

Review of Risk Components[3]

A company faces many different risk factors, which could have an impact on the how attractive an investment is in a particular company. Each of these factors should be analyzed and addressed during a valuation. We generally assign five levels of risk to each component: low, medium-low, medium, medium-high, and high. In reviewing Potter, we assigned the risk assessments to the company as shown in Exhibit 20.

Exhibit 20. Risk Assessment for Potter

Risk	Impact
Economic	Low
Business	Low to Medium
Operating	Low to Medium
Financial	Low to Medium
Asset	Low to Medium
Product	Medium to High
Market	High
Technology	Medium to High
Regulatory	Medium to High
Legal	Medium to High

Conclusion of Comparative Industry Analysis

The company's balance sheet generally compares unfavorably to its peer group, due to its slightly stronger current assets and weaker equity balances, as well as its high levels of debt.

The company compares favorably in measures of profitability, which is of importance to investors. The company's financial and operating ratios yield mixed to negative results when compared to the industry as a whole.

Overall, a comparison of the company to others in its industry produces negative results. This will have a negative influence on the value of the subject interest in the company.

Valuation Methods

Asset Approach

The asset approach considers the tangible net asset value of the enterprise's assets and liabilities under conditions of an orderly liquidation. The normal procedure is to adjust each item on the company's balance sheet to reflect the cash result of an orderly liquidation. Transaction costs are factored into the value and are thus calculated.

Application of the asset approach requires an analysis of the company's assets and liabilities. "The value-basis balance sheet may be materially different from the cost-basis balance sheet in two ways:

3 Key discussions from this section are obtained from *Understanding Business Valuation: A Practical Guide to Valuing Small to Medium Size Businesses,* 5th edition, by Gary R. Trugman (Wiley, 2017).

- "The balances in the asset and liability accounts have been revalued; and
- "Several new asset and liability accounts may be added."[4]

The first step in applying the asset approach is to create a balance sheet including all assets and liabilities at historical cost.

Exhibit 21 displays the balance sheet as of Dec. 31, 2017, as reported on Potter's 2017 tax return.

Exhibit 21. Potter's LLC Balance Sheet	
	Historical Costs ($) Dec. 31, 2017
Assets	
Current Assets	
Cash	6,173,400
Accounts receivable, net	7,583,300
Costs and estimated earnings in excess of billings	1,152,500
Restricted cash	17,743,100
Prepaid and other assets	124,200
Total Current Assets	32,776,500
Property, Plant and Equipment, Net	
Property, plant and equipment	1,448,800
Accumulated depreciation	(160,300)
Total Property, Plant and Equipment, Net	1,288,500
Total Assets	34,065,000
Liabilities and Stockholder's Equity	
Current Liabilities	
Accounts payable and accruals	7,686,100
Current portion of long-term debt	33,400
Notes payable—line of credit	4,326,400
Billings in excess of costs and estimated earnings	5,872,000
Shareholder loan	2,000,000
Other current liabilities	10,035,400
Total Current Liabilities	29,953,300
Long-Term Liabilities	
Long-term debt	768,900
Total Long-Term Liabilities	768,900
Total Liabilities	30,722,200
Total Stockholder's Equity	3,342,800
Total Liabilities and Stockholder's Equity	34,065,000

4 S.P. Pratt and A.V. Niculita, *Valuing a Business: The Analysis and Appraisal of Closely Held Companies*, New York: McGraw-Hill, 2008, pg. 351.

The next step in the asset approach is to determine which assets and liabilities require an adjustment. Based on discussions with management and the analysis that is reported on herein, the following accounts have been restated to fair market value:

- *Shareholder loans.* Loans from the shareholders are presented on the balance sheet as liabilities. Based on discussions with management, Katerina Potter and Damon Potter put in the loans equally in 2013. The amounts have not been paid back, and, according to management, they have no intention of having the company pay them back. Therefore, we have reclassified it to equity as a capital contribution the owners made.

- Based on discussions with management, and an analysis of the supporting documents, all other accounts are reported at their fair market value and do not require an adjustment.

Exhibit 22 on the next page shows the historical balance sheet as of Dec. 31, 2017, compared to the fair market values at Dec. 31, 2017.

Thus, using the asset approach, we believe the value for a 100% controlling, marketable interest in Potter is approximately $5,342,800 (see "Total Stockholder's Equity" line in Exhibit 22).

In the valuation of any business ownership interest, it is incumbent upon the valuation analyst to consider whether the business enterprise is worth more in liquidation than it is as a going concern. In liquidation, the company would perform the following: (i) sell all its assets; (ii) collect what it is owed from its assets; and (iii) pay off all its debts. This approach would typically set the floor value as the appraiser would treat the company as if it were going out of business. As a going concern, the company assumes it will continue to operate into the future and will, therefore, continue to have a stream of income and cash flows. Over time, the value of the income and cash flows would be worth more than if the company was to liquidate. As a result, Potter is an operating company and is worth more as a going concern than it would be in liquidation. In addition, the asset approach method presumes the ability of the hypothetical willing buyer to convert the entity's net assets into cash. In this case, the owner of a noncontrolling interest in Potter does not have that power without the consent of a sufficient number of other shareholders. For these reasons, the asset approach was rejected in valuing the interest in Potter.

Market Approach

The market approach is a process for comparing prices paid in transactions for comparable businesses that have a satisfactory degree of similarity to the subject enterprise. This approach

Exhibit 22. Historical Balance Sheet Compared to Fair Market Values			
	Historical Costs ($) Dec. 31, 2017	Adjustments ($)	Adjusted Costs ($) Dec. 31, 2017
Assets			
Current Assets			
Cash	6,173,400	-	6,173,400
Accounts receivable, net	7,583,300	-	7,583,300
Costs and estimated earnings in excess of billings	1,152,500	-	1,152,500
Restricted cash	17,743,100	-	17,743,100
Prepaid and other assets	124,200	-	124,200
Total Current Assets	32,776,500	-	32,776,500
Property, Plant and Equipment, Net			
Property, plant and equipment	1,448,800	-	1,448,800
Accumulated depreciation	(160,300)	-	(160,300)
Total Property, Plant and Equipment, Net	1,288,500	-	1,288,500
Total Assets	34,065,000		34,065,000
Liabilities and Stockholder's Equity			
Current Liabilities			
Accounts payable and accruals	7,686,100		7,686,100
Current portion of long-term debt	33,400	-	33,400
Notes payable—line of credit	4,326,400	-	4,326,400
Billings in excess of costs and estimated earnings	5,872,000	-	5,872,000
Shareholder loan	2,000,000	(2,000,000)	-
Other current liabilities	10,035,400	-	10,035,400
Total Current Liabilities	29,953,300	(2,000,000)	27,953,300
Long-Term Liabilities			
Long-term debt	768,900	-	768,900
Total Long-Term Liabilities	768,900	-	768,900
Total Liabilities	30,722,200	(2,000,000)	28,722,200
Total Stockholder's Equity	3,342,800	2,000,000	5,342,800
Total Liabilities and Stockholder's Equity	$34,065,000		$34,065,000

is based on the principle of substitution, which implies that the market value is equal to the cost to buy a comparable substitute. Comparable transactions can be stock exchange transactions of public companies or the sales of a small private business in a negotiated transaction.

We searched for private and public companies similar to Potter and conferred with management regarding potential comparable company data using the following transaction databases:

1. DealStats (M&A method); and

2. BIZCOMPS (M&A method).

An initial search of the databases for NAICS codes 236115, 236116, and 236220 and SIC codes 1521, 1522, and 1542 produced the following number of transactions:

Database	Number of Transactions
DealStats	165
BIZCOMPS	101

We then applied the following criteria to narrow down our initial search:

1. *Revenue range.* We looked for revenues within the range of $1.0 million to $100 million.

2. *Date range.* All dates prior to Dec. 31, 2017 (the valuation date);

3. *Location.* Companies located in the United States;

4. *Transaction type.* We searched all asset sales;

5. *Business description.* Residential and commercial construction companies.

6. *Other.* We searched for anomalies including companies with negative net income or equity, etc.

Based on our search and the criteria discussed above, we were left with the following number of transactions:

Database	Number of Transactions
DealStats	25
BIZCOMPS	13

We found a sufficient number of transactions of private companies in DealStats and BIZCOMPS and have applied the market approach using these databases.

DealStats Database. DealStats determines the value of a business as follows:

Subject Company Revenue or Earnings
x Pricing Multiple (as selected by appraiser)
= Indicated Market Value of Invested Capital
+ Assets not included in the multiple (usually AR and cash)
- Liabilities excluded from the multiple (usually all)
+ Real Estate
+ Non-operating assets
- Non-operating liabilities
= Indicated value of equity

A review of DealStats produced the results shown in Exhibit 23.

Our analysis of Potter indicates that the company compares below its industry peers. Therefore, we have used the harmonic mean multiple (see last line of Exhibit 23). We selected the harmonic mean because it is our opinion that, when price is the numerator, the harmonic mean is a better measure of central tendency for valuation multiples than the mean.

Exhibit 23. DealStats Valuation Multiples for Comparable Companies to Potter					
MVIC to:	Net Sales	Gross Profit	EBITDA	EBIT	Discretionary Earnings
# of Transactions	25.00	25.00	25.00	24.00	25.00
High	0.85	2.67	11.87	12.32	6.80
Low	0.08	0.34	0.69	1.01	0.60
Standard Deviation	0.24	0.63	2.82	2.87	1.31
Mean	0.38	1.09	4.34	4.72	2.54
Coefficient of Variation	0.63	0.58	0.65	0.61	0.52
Upper Quartile	0.85	2.67	11.87	12.32	6.80
Median	0.36	1.07	3.56	3.77	2.67
Lower Quartile	0.20	0.60	2.23	2.61	1.55
Harmonic Mean	0.24	0.78	2.64	3.15	1.89

Using the harmonic mean multiples and Potter's adjusted income base at Dec. 31, 2017, the indication of value is $8,767,000 as shown in Exhibit 24.

Exhibit 24. Indications of Value for Potter Using DealStats						
Valuation Multiple	Count of Multiples	Coefficient of Variation	Valuation Multiples	Value From Multiples ($)	Select Percentage	Value ($)
MVIC/Net Sales	25.00	0.63	0.24	9,155,700	20%	1,831,100
MVIC/Gross Profit	25.00	0.58	0.78	3,994,100	20%	798,800
MVIC/EBIT	24.00	0.61	3.15	11,805,100	20%	2,361,000
MVIC/EBITDA	25.00	0.65	2.64	10,043,700	20%	2,008,700
MVIC/Discretionary Earnings	25.00	0.52	1.89	8,836,900	20%	1,767,400
					100%	
Indicated Market Value of Invested Capital						8,767,000

The pricing multiple represents the prices paid for the net operating assets of the company. However, we are valuing the equity of the company, which includes all of the assets and all of the liabilities. Accordingly, we must adjust the value indication derived above, which is an asset sale indication of value, to an indication of value for the equity of Potter.

Using the description of a typical asset sale discussed above, the following assets and liabilities, as of Dec. 31, 2017, would not transfer in the type of sale the DealStats database represents. See Exhibit 25.

Exhibit 25. Summary of Potter's Current Assets and Liabilities	
Cash	$6,173,400
Accounts receivable, net	7,583,300
Restricted cash	17,743,100
Costs and estimated earnings in excess of billings	1,152,500
Accounts payable and accruals	(7,686,100)
Current portion of long-term debt	(33,400)
Notes payable—line of credit	(4,326,400)
Billings in excess of costs and estimated earnings	(5,872,000)
Other current liabilities	(10,035,400)
Long-term debt	(768,900)
Total	**$3,930,100**

Accordingly, the indication of value for Potter, using the M&A method, employing the DealStats database and adjusting for the reasons discussed above, is $12,697,100 (see Exhibit 26).

Exhibit 26. Indication of Value for Potter	
Asset sale indication of value	$8,767,000
Adjustment of asset sale to equity	$3,930,100
Indication of value	$12,697,100

The use of the DealStats transaction database yields an indication of value for a noncontrolling interest because it is based on the revenue transactions for a noncontrolling interest in the underlying companies. It is also an indication of value for a marketable interest because the pricing multiples are derived from transactions that took place between a buyer and a seller who were fully cognizant of the fact that the ownership interest had changed hands. Accordingly, the value indication is for a noncontrolling interest, on a marketable basis.

BIZCOMPS Database. The BIZCOMPS database determines the value of a business as follows:

Subject Company Revenue or Earnings
x Pricing Multiple (as selected by appraiser)
= Indicated Market Value of Invested Capital
+ Assets not included in the multiple (usually AR and cash)
- Liabilities excluded from the multiple (usually all)
+ Real Estate
+ Non-operating assets
- Non-operating liabilities
= Indicated value of equity

Exhibit 27. BIZCOMPS Valuation Multiples for Comparable Companies to Potter		
Price to:	Net Sales	Discretionary Earnings
# of Transactions	13.00	13.00
High	0.48	3.15
Low	0.21	1.08
Standard Deviation	0.09	0.65
Mean	0.31	2.37
Coefficient of Variation	0.28	0.28
Upper Quartile	0.48	3.15
Median	0.28	2.48
Lower Quartile	0.24	1.85
Harmonic Mean	0.29	2.16

A review of the BIZCOMPS database produced the results shown in Exhibit 27.

Using the harmonic mean multiples from BIZCOMPS and Potter's adjusted income base as of Dec. 31, 2017, we derived the indications of value of $10,519,400 shown in Exhibit 28.

Accordingly, the indication of value for Potter, using the M&A method and employing the BIZCOMPS database and adjusting for the reasons discussed above, is $14,449,500 (see Exhibit 29).

Exhibit 28. Indications of Value for Potter Using BIZCOMPS						
Valuation Multiple	Count of Multiples	Coefficient of Variation	Valuation Multiples	Value From Multiples ($)	Select Percentage	Value ($)
Sale Price/Annual Gross	13.00	0.28	0.29	10,944,900	50%	5,472,500
Sale Price/SDE	13.00	0.28	2.16	10,093,800	50%	5,046,900
					100%	
Indicated Market Value of Invested Capital						10,519,400

Use of the BIZCOMPS transaction database yields an indication of value for a noncontrolling interest because it is based on transactions for a noncontrolling interest in the underlying companies. It is also an indication of value for a marketable interest because the pricing multiples are for transactions that took place between a buyer and a seller who were fully cognizant of the fact that the ownership interest had changed hands. Accordingly, the value indication is for a noncontrolling interest, on a marketable basis.

Exhibit 29. Indication of Value for Potter	
Asset sale indication of value	$10,519,400
Adjustment of asset sale to equity	$3,930,100
Indication of value	$14,449,500

Reconciliation of the Market Approach

Based on our detailed review of the underlying transactions and the proximity in value, we have determined that an equal weighting of 50% to the value arrived at using the DealStats database and a 50% weighting to the value arrived at using the BIZCOMPS database was appropriate (see Exhibit 30). Therefore, the preliminary value before discounts for Potter is $13,573,400.

Exhibit 30. Summary of Values Using the Market Approach			
	Value ($)	Weight	Value ($)
DealStats	12,697,100	50.0%	6,348,600
BIZCOMPS	14,449,500	50.0%	7,224,800
Preliminary value before discounts			13,573,400

Income Approach—Discounted Cash Flow Method

The income approach is the capitalization of anticipated earnings at an appropriate capitalization rate with respect to the anticipated risk of the enterprise. The income approach is based on the premise that a prudent investor would pay no more for an investment than he or she would for an alternative investment with similar characteristics of risk and return.

The discounted cash flow (DCF) method is an income approach whereby the present value of future expected net cash flows is calculated using a discount rate. To estimate a value using the DCF method, the significant inputs include:

- A projection of future net cash flows (NCF) over several periods;
- A residual or "terminal" value at the end of the projected period; and
- A discount rate used to determine the present value of both the future cash flows and terminal values.

$$PV = \frac{NCF_1}{(1+r)^{0.5}} + \frac{NCF_2}{(1+r)^{1.5}} + \frac{NCF_3}{(1+r)^{2.5}} + \frac{NCF_4}{(1+r)^{3.5}} + \cdots + \frac{NCF_f}{(1+r)^{f-0.5}} + \frac{NCF_f * (1+g)/(r-g)}{(1+r)^{f-0.5}}$$

Where:

PV = present value

NCF = net cash flow

f = final year of projection

g = growth

r = discount rate

The assumption is midyear discounting as NCF occurs evenly through the year and that the discounting begins at the first day of the first year.

Net Cash Flow

NCF to the invested capital holders considers sales and all expenses including taxes and other cash expenditures such as interest and principal payments to debt holders, new sources of debt financing, working capital needs, and capital expenditures.

The DCF method requires judgment in estimating many model parameters such as future revenue growth rates, debt servicing, discount rates, profit margins, and capital requirements. In addition, it is important to support these assumptions with historical data and/or industry projections, and possibly peer performance and to support the DCF valuation outcome.

The formula used to derive NCF to invested capital is:

$$NCF = EBIT\ (\text{tax affected}) - CAPEX + DA - (+)\ \Delta WC$$

Where:
DA = depreciation and amortization
EBIT = earnings before interest and taxes
ΔWC = the change in working capital
CAPEX = expenditures for capital equipment

Revenue Growth Rates

Potter's average CAGR was 45.1% in sales achieved from 2012 through 2017. First Research,[5] a market research tool, predicts that the commercial construction industry will grow by a CAGR of 7% and a CAGR of 4% for residential construction through 2022. In addition to using First Research, we also interviewed management and performed a thorough analysis of its current backlog, estimated backlog, and bid proposals that were submitted and still outstanding. Based on all of this information, revenues during the projection period are expected to grow by 5.5% per year through 2022, and then by 3% into perpetuity, which is equal to the long-term expected rate of inflation.

Gross Profit

Based on discussions with management and a review of the estimated gross profit and all open and estimated projects, gross profit is projected to remain at 13.6% for the foreseeable future, which is in line with the gross profit percentage in 2017.

Operating Expenses

Based on discussions with management and a review of the company's financial information, the following projections were made:

5 Available at bvresources.com/firstresearch.

- Rent was estimated to be $40,000 based on an analysis of reasonable rents and discussions with real estate brokers.

- As previously discussed, we have researched the ERI database for the average salaries for a president and a vice president in the residential and commercial construction industry in the New York statewide region for a company with revenues equal to Potter's projected revenues in 2018. As such, we have estimated salaries for a president at $604,300 and a vice president at $295,500.

- All other operating expenses are projected to grow by 3%, which is equal to the average long-term inflation rate.

Tax Expense

Although the company is a pass-through entity and does not pay taxes in the same manner as a C corporation, we deducted taxes from the earnings before taxes as if the company was a C corporation. We estimated that the company would have an effective tax rate of 20.93% (see Exhibit 31).

Exhibit 31. Delaware Chancery Model for Projected Period

	C Corp.	S Corp.	S Corp. Valuation
Income before tax	$100.00	$100.00	$100.00
Corporate tax rate	27.92%	0.00%	**20.93%**
Available earnings	$72.08	$100.00	$79.07
Dividend or personal income tax rate (federal and state)	32.62%	38.42%	32.62%
Differential between corporate and personal rates			-10.50%
Available after dividends	$48.57	$61.58	$61.58

It is important to note the tax rate in Exhibit 31 for a pass-through entity of 20.93% to be used in the years after 2018 is based on the Delaware Chancery model for a company that is located on Long Island, N.Y., including the appropriate rate and tax effective rates for the federal, state, and MTA surcharge. In addition, this entity qualified for the QBI deduction so that was taken into account when determining the above-tax rate for a pass-through entity. Every state and jurisdiction would need to compute the tax rate for a pass-through entity using the appropriate and applicable tax and effective tax rates, as well as to determine whether the business qualifies for the QBI deduction.

Profit Margins

Profitability is measured by the pretax earnings. As a result of the preceding assumptions, pretax income is expected to be approximately 8.2% of revenues in 2018 and grow to 10.1% of revenues by 2022. Pretax earnings are expected to remain at this level for the foreseeable future based on the company's historical data and the projections discussed above. This excludes any extraordinary and one-time expenses as previously discussed.

Depreciation and Amortization

Depreciation and amortization expenses are not included in the estimation of free cash flows because they are not cash expenditures. Therefore, depreciation and amortization are added back to pretax income to derive free cash flows. We have projected depreciation expense assuming that the existing asset base has about five years of remaining depreciable life. We have also assumed that all future capital expenditures will have, on average, 10-year lives.

Capital Expenditures

Capital expenditures are cash outflows that must be forecasted in each year in order to derive free cash flows. In general, as any company grows, it will need more capital to sustain increased demand for its products. Thus, we link the amount of capital expenditures that will be incurred in each forecast year to the amount of revenues in that same year. In other words, capital expenditures are estimated as a percentage of revenues in each projected year, and, as revenues increase, capital expenditures also increase at the same rate. Based on discussions with management and an analysis of the historical capital expenditures, we project capital expenditures to be $258,500 in 2018, which is equal to the five-year historical average. This figure grows by the same rate as revenues each year thereafter.

Change in Working Capital

Similar to capital expenditures, most companies must maintain higher levels of working capital to support growth. Therefore, we also examine the historic rate of changes in working capital that are associated with changes in revenues to make assumptions about what that rate will be going forward. Also similar to capital expenditures, the rate of increase in working capital will be proportional to the rate of increase in projected revenues. Working capital was projected based on the projected balance sheet and income statement as well as the expected changes in the company's working capital needs.

Terminal Value and Stabilized Growth Rate

In theory, the DCF model incorporates NCF that will be generated in the next period and in all future periods into perpetuity. However, from a practical point of view, the model must incorporate a given duration at which time the value of all the future cash flows from that point on and into infinity are collapsed into one value known as the terminal value.

Therefore, we selected a 3.0% annual revenue growth assumption for the terminal period, which is equal to the long-term historical inflation rate.

Application of the Build-Up Method

In the build-up method, different components of rates of return are summed in order to build up a rate of return appropriate for an investment in a small, privately held company.

The process begins with a rate of return on an investment that is considered to be free from the risk of default, or a so-called risk-free rate. A series of incremental rates of return are then added to the risk-free rate to incorporate the additional risks that come with an investment in the equities of small, privately held companies.

Using the Duff and Phelps Navigator, we have arrived at a discount rate of 16% before the addition of a company-specific risk percentage. Based on the discussions throughout this chapter regarding the company and the risk factors, we have added a company-specific risk of 5% to the 16% discount rate to arrive at a total discount rate of 21%.

Discounted Cash Flows Method—Indication of Value

To utilize a discount rate within the DCF method, the rate is converted to a present value interest factor (PVIF) using the following formula:

$$PVIF = \frac{1}{(1+r)^t}$$

Where
r = discount rate
t = future period that cash is received

NCF is expected to continue beyond the projection period, and this value is referred to as a "terminal value." A terminal value is calculated by dividing the next year's expected cash flow by a "capitalization rate," which is the difference between the discount rate and the expected growth into perpetuity. Consequently, this model, known as the Gordon growth model, calculates a value into perpetuity. The following formula expresses the model:

$$V = \frac{NCF\ x\ (1 + g)}{(r - g)}$$

Where
V = value
r = discount rate
g = stabilized growth into perpetuity
NCF = stabilized net cash flow

Using the concluded discount rate of 21% and a terminal growth rate (g) of 3.0%, the resulting capitalization rate is 18%. Therefore, the future terminal value is approximately $13,361,500. This figure represents the value after the projection period discounted back to today's value.

This indication of value arrived at under the discounted cash flow method of the income approach yields an indication of value for a noncontrolling interest on an as if freely traded marketable basis because it is based on the cash flows available to a noncontrolling owner and on rates of return on investments with those characteristics.

Discounts and Premiums

Discounts and premiums are used in valuations to assist the appraiser in arriving at the appropriate concluded value. For example, if the approach and method selected arrive at a controlling and marketable value and the required value needs to be on a noncontrolling and nonmarketable basis, then the appraiser would need to apply both a discount for lack of control and a discount for lack of marketability.

Discounts and premiums are usually expressed as a percentage of some base value, with the discount or premium subtracted from or added to that base value. The adjustment should reflect the differences between the characteristics of the interest being valued and those of the group upon which the indication of value is based. These differences in characteristics create differences in risk—either to the entity or to its owner—whether the differences arise from contingent liabilities, lack of control, lack of marketability, or some other factor. A discount represents an increase in yield to compensate an investor for the increase in risk for their investment.

Adjustment for Lack of Control

It is well established that a company's control owners have rights that minority owners do not and that the differences in those rights—and, perhaps more importantly, how those rights are exercised and to what economic benefit—cause a differential in the per-share value of a control ownership block versus a minority ownership block. The value of control depends not only on legal power and rights, but also on economic potential. This lack of control is generally referred to as a "minority interest." It is defined as "an ownership interest of less than 50% of the voting interest in a business enterprise."

All of the empirical data for guidance in quantifying minority discounts and control premiums come from the public markets for stocks or partnership interests. These empirical data fall broadly into two categories:

- Premiums paid for acquisitions of companies compared with public-market minority trading prices prior to the acquisition announcement; and
- Where net asset value is known or reasonably estimated, the percentage discount observed in minority interest transactions compared with the underlying net asset value.

According to the *FactSet Mergerstat/BVR Control Premium Study* Frequently Asked Questions,[6] "[t]he minority discount is widely perceived of as the inverse of the control premium, where an acquirer would assumingly pay a higher price for control in a company and pay a lesser amount for a minority stake."

Further, the database uses the following calculation:

$$\text{Implied minority discount} = 1 - [1/(1 + \text{control premium})]$$

An alternate equation that can be used to determine the implied median minority discount (where CP is the control premium) is:

$$\text{Implied median minority discount} = CP/(1 + CP)$$

Thus, we have applied a discount for lack of control of 11.2% to our valuation of Potter.

6 bvresources.com/products/faqs/factset-mergerstat-bvr-control-premium-study.

Adjustment for Lack of Marketability/Illiquidity

It is commonly recognized and well documented that an interest that is not readily marketable generally trades at a price lower than a similar interest that is readily marketable. When an ownership interest lacks certain elements of marketability, an adjustment to preliminary value is generally appropriate. This adjustment is commonly referred to as the discount for lack of marketability (DLOM).

Market-based methods are often computed using data from studies of securities traded on national exchanges. There are, however, certain marketability differences between an investment in a company and publicly traded securities. An owner of publicly traded securities can know at all times the market value of his or her holding. The investor can sell that holding on virtually a moment's notice and receive cash, net of brokerage fees, within several working days. Such is not so in the Potter case. Consequently, liquidating a position in the company would be a more costly and time-consuming process than liquidating an investment in a publicly traded company.

Several recognized studies review the price differentials between restricted and nonrestricted shares of corporate stock. Since the restricted corporate stock is illiquid for a period of several years, the differential in price between the restricted and nonrestricted shares offers evidence on discounts related to lack of marketability. These studies cover several hundred transactions that occurred between 1966 and 2017.

In arriving at an appropriate DLOM, we have considered several methods. Specifically, we addressed the general benchmark restricted stock and initial public offering (IPO) studies. In addition to the empirical data, we have considered the factors the U.S. Tax Court analyzed in *Mandelbaum* (69 TCM 2852; 1995), see Exhibit 32, as well as the Stout Restricted Stock Study,[7] see Exhibit 33, to name a few.

Exhibit 32 shows just a few of the factors considered and the impact they have on marketability of Potter.

Exhibit 32. *Mandelbaum* Factors

Factor	Effect on Discount for Marketability
Private vs. Public Sales of Stock	Increase
Financial Statement Analysis	Increase
Company Distribution Policy	Decrease
Nature of the Company	Decrease
The Company's History	Decrease
The Company's Position in the Industry	Increase
The Company's Position in the Economy	Decrease
Company's Management	Increase
Amount of Control in Transferred Shares	Decrease
Restriction on Transferability	Increase
Holding Period	Increase
Company's Redemption Policy	Increase

7 bvresources.com/stout.

Exhibit 33 shows the summary and conclusion as it appears in the calculation as performed using the Stout Restricted Stock Study.

Exhibit 33. Stout Restricted Stock Study	
Summary and Conclusion	
Restricted Stock Equivalent Discount	
Financial Characteristics Comparison (Weighted Average)	18.50%
Best Comparable Analysis (Range)	14.7%-24.0%
Selected Restricted Stock Equivalent Discount	18.50%
Times: Selected Market Volatility Adjustment Factor	1.25
Adjusted Restricted Stock Equivalent Discount	23.10%
Selected Private Equity Discount	43.90%

Concluded Discount

We have, therefore, concluded that the appropriate DLOM for the subject interest in Potter is 23.1%.

Reconciliation of Values

The preliminary values derived throughout this case study, including an appropriate discount for lack of control (11.2%) and discount for marketability (23.1%), are summarized in Exhibit 34.

Exhibit 34. Value Indications for Potter	
Value Indications	
Asset approach	$3,648,400
Income approach	$11,927,700
Market approach	$9,268,800

We believe the value of the subject interest (Potter LLC) should be a blend of the indications of value developed from the various methods. For a noncontrolling investor in an operating company, the primary investment objective is the annual cash flow. If a particular investment generates healthy annual cash flows, this minimizes a noncontrolling investor's concerns regarding the unknown time horizon for the ultimate liquidation of the entity and a distribution of the proceeds. Therefore, we believe the income approach produces the most appropriate indication of value, followed by the market approach, with no consideration of the asset approach for the following reasons:

- The main focus of the income approach is future cash flows (the anticipated future income from distributions or capital gains that can be reasonably expected). This is very important to both current and future investors.

- The market approach relies on pricing multiples of companies whose degree of similarity or comparability to Potter and applying it to a historical earnings stream.

These transactions are sometimes reported without all the needed information to fully determine what actually transpired or whether there was a synergistic sale. Nevertheless, it is using recent transactions of similar companies, and we can take some measures to help eliminate these issues if the pool of transactions is large enough and if we use statistical metrics (i.e., coefficient of variation). Therefore, we have considered it in our conclusion of value as a secondary and supportive approach to the income approach.

- The asset approach is more appropriate and applicable when valuing a controlling interest, in liquidation, or when the sale of the entity is imminent as the subject's ownership should be able to cause the sale of the company's assets. This is not the case in this valuation.

Conclusion of Value

We have, therefore, assigned a weighting of 75% to the income approach and a weighting of 25% to the market approach in determining our final conclusion of value for a 1% interest to be $112,600, as shown in Exhibit 35.

Exhibit 35. Conclusion of Value for Potter

Valuation Method	Value	Basis	DLOC	Minority, Marketable Value	DLOM	Minority, Nonmarketable Value	Weighting[1]
Asset Approach:	$5,342,800	Control, Marketable	11.2%	$4,744,400	23.1%	$3,648,400	0%
Income Approach: Discounted Cash Flow Method	$17,466,900	Control, Marketable	11.2%	$15,510,600	23.1%	$11,927,700	75%
Market Approach[2]:	$13,573,300	Control, Marketable	11.2%	$12,053,100	23.1%	$9,268,800	25%
DealStats	$12,697,100	Control, Marketable					
BIZCOMPS	$14,449,500	Control, Marketable					
Indicated fair market value of a 100% interest on noncontrolling, nonmarketable basis						$11,263,000	
Fair market value of a 1% interest on noncontrolling, nonmarketable basis						$112,600	

Notes:

[1] Asset approach is discounted to 0% weighting because it is inapplicable to use when valuing an operating company that is treated as a going concern.

[2] Market approach is weighted based on an analysis of the databases as follows:
DealStats—50%
BIZCOMPS—50%

SECTION II:
CURRENT MARKET AND TRENDS FOR RESIDENTIAL AND NONRESIDENTIAL CONSTRUCTION COMPANIES

5. Current Market for Residential and Commercial Building Contractors

By Pasquale Rafanelli

The economy, industry, and current market all play important roles in the future of a company. This is no different for residential and commercial building businesses, which are often heavily dependent on individuals, the public sector, and business investment in new infrastructure and maintenance of existing infrastructure.

This chapter features a summary of the current market for residential and commercial building contractors, along with a summary of the construction market overall.

Construction Market Overall

Dodge Data & Analytics recently released its "2020 Dodge Construction Outlook."[1] The report predicts that total U.S. construction starts will slip to $776 billion in 2020, a decline of 4% from the 2019 estimated level.

"The recovery in construction starts that began during 2010 in the aftermath of the Great Recession is coming to an end," states Richard Branch, chief economist for Dodge Data & Analytics. "Easing economic growth driven by mounting trade tensions and lack of skilled labor will lead to a broad based, but orderly pullback in overall construction starts in 2020. After increasing 3% in 2018, construction starts dipped an estimated 1% in 2019 and will fall

1 www.construction.com/news/Construction-Starts-Slip-back-2020-Dodge-Data-Analytics.

4% in 2020." He goes on to say, "Economic growth is slowing but is not anticipated to contract next year. Construction starts, therefore, will decline but the level of activity will remain close to recent highs. By major construction sector, the dollar value of starts for residential buildings will be down 6%, while starts for nonresidential buildings will drop 3%."

Dodge Data & Analytics also reports that the pattern of construction starts for more specific segments is as follows:

- The dollar value of single-family housing starts will be down 3% in 2020, and the number of units will also drop 5%, to 765,000 (Dodge basis). Affordability issues and the tight supply of entry-level homes have kept home demand low and buyers uninspired.

- Multifamily construction was a leader in the recovery, with eight years of growth since 2009. However, multifamily vacancy rates have remained static over the past year, suggesting slower economic growth in 2020. Multifamily starts are predicted to drop 13% in dollars and 15% in units, to 410,000 (Dodge basis).

- The dollar value of commercial building starts will drop 6% in 2020. The steepest declines will occur in commercial warehouses and hotels, while the decline in office construction will be tempered by high-value data center construction.

- In 2020, institutional construction starts will remain even with the 2019 level as the influence of public dollars adds stability to the forecast. Education building and health facility starts should continue to see modest growth next year, offset by declines in recreation and transportation buildings.

- The dollar value of manufacturing plant construction will fall 2% in 2020 following an estimated decline of 29% in 2019. Rising trade tensions have negatively impacted this sector as recent data, both domestic and global, suggest the manufacturing sector is contracting.

- Public works construction starts will rise 4% in 2020, with growth continuing across all project types. Recent federal appropriations have kept funding for public works construction either steady or slightly higher, which has equated to continued growth in environmental and transportation infrastructure starts.

The following sections break down the factors that influence growth for each of the residential building and the commercial building sectors of the market.

Residential Building Contractors

Vertical IQ,[2] a market research platform, projects 4.01% compounded annual growth for residential building contractors from 2017 to 2023, which is slower than the growth of the overall economy (see Exhibit 1).

Of course, several factors affect the growth in the residential building market including the following:

- *Housing market recovery.* The housing market strengthened from 2012 through 2018 and leveled off somewhat in 2019. While many builders report increased traffic, construction and sales of new homes are hampered by tight credit and a shortage of workers and lots. Single-family construction starts grew 8.6% in 2017 and 4% in the first 10 months of 2018. Multiunit construction declined 10% in 2017, but grew 8% in the first 10 months of 2018. Dodge Analytics forecasts a 3% drop in single-family starts in

2 Vertical IQ Inc. is an industry research resource available at bvresources.com/verticaliq. Its industry information is reprinted with permission.

Exhibit 1. Residential Building Contractors Industry Growth

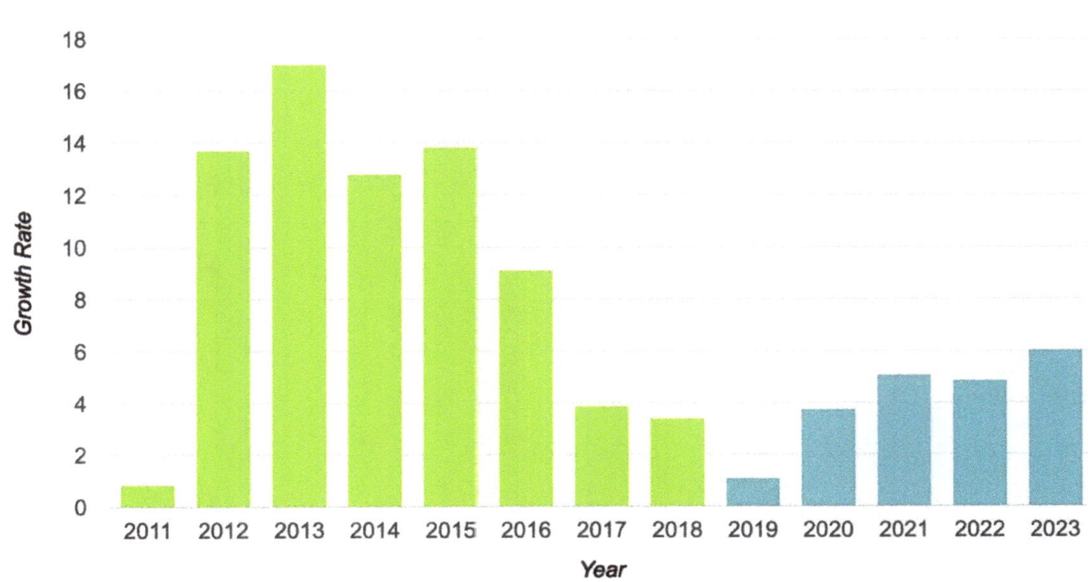

2019, along with an 8% decline in multiunit starts, which it predicts will further decline in 2020. Additionally, there will be a slight decline in homebuyer demand as a result of higher mortgage rates, diminished affordability, and reduced tax advantages for home ownership as the result of tax reform.

- *Housing starts.* Housing starts are an important indicator of the level of new single-family home construction. Generally, the number of housing starts rises along with demand for homes, which results from increased individual wealth, consumer confidence, and access to credit. According to the *Economic Outlook Update,*[3] single-family housing will be unchanged in terms of dollars, alongside a 3% drop in housing starts, to 815,000 (Dodge basis).

- *Thirty-year conventional mortgage rate.* The 30-year fixed mortgage rate is the most common type of loan for home purchases in the U.S. Lower interest rates and credit standards increase the ability of individuals to purchase property. In 2019, the 30-year conventional mortgage rate was expected to remain low.

- *Unemployment rate.* An individual's ability to buy a house depends on income. When unemployment levels rise, homeownership decreases because buyers cannot afford to make large investments. According to the *Economic Outlook Update*, the national unemployment rate is expected to stay at or near historic 50-year lows in 2019 and 2020, which is favorable to the residential construction market.

- *Strong remodeling.* As the economy and job markets have improved, spending on remodeling has increased but represents a smaller percentage of private construction spending. Remodeling as a percentage of overall spending reached a recent high of 49.5% in 2011 but fell to a low of 35% in 2015 and 2016 as spending shifted to new home construction. Remodeling spending grew 10% to 11% annually in 2014 to 2016, then jumped 19% in 2017, to account for 37% of total residential construction spending. Remodeling activity is forecast to grow about 6% to 7% in 2019. Popular remodeling projects involve bathrooms, kitchens, bedrooms, flooring, and roofs, although demand for smaller projects is growing.

- *Foreclosures affect demand.* The volume of foreclosed residential properties is on the downturn. Foreclosure filings hit an historic norm of about 1% in 2013 but were back

3 The *Economic Outlook Update* is published monthly and quarterly by Business Valuation Resources. It is available at bvresources.com/eou.

up to 8% by the end of 2015, according to RealtyTrac. Foreclosures took another dive, falling 17% at the end of 2016, 25% at the close of 2017, and 19% at the end of 2018. As the inventory of foreclosed properties has declined, the price of homes has increased, rising 2% in 2015, 4.6% in 2016, 5% in 2017, and 0.3% in the first nine months in 2018.

As reported by Vertical IQ, the following trends will have an impact on the residential construction industry and can also be seen as market opportunities.

- *Potential in active adult housing.* Attractive demographics and pent-up demand are projected to help drive the active adult housing market, which includes age-qualified residences. The population of adults age 65 and older is estimated to grow more than 35% over the next decade. Recovering stock portfolios have improved consumer confidence among retirees, and many buyers have been waiting out the housing market for several years in hopes of better market conditions. Activity is increasing in developments with fewer amenities, which charge lower homeowner fees. While financing continues to be an industrywide problem, only 40% of buyers in age-qualified communities require mortgages.

- *Focus on community and smaller developments.* After getting burned during the most recent recession, investors are shying away from large-scale/master-planned developments. Demand is increasing for smaller infill projects and groups of homes in established areas. Abandoned shopping centers, strip malls, and big box parking lots located close to heavily populated areas are ideal redevelopment opportunities. Communities with high "walkability" ratings appeal to buyers looking for an urban lifestyle without big-city hassles and prices.

- *Low-cost green housing.* While green building is becoming more mainstream, implementation of environmentally friendly features in residential construction is occurring on a smaller scale. Most buyers are unwilling to give up style, function, or value when considering green building. Energy efficiency, water-saving, and healthy-home features are popular options. Likely green building materials include low-E windows, engineered lumber, and water-efficient fixtures.

- *Multigenerational housing opportunities.* A significant percentage of homeowners are expecting to move into larger houses or add on to existing houses to accommodate children and aging parents moving in. The shift to multigenerational housing arrangements is due partly to economic and financial conditions and partly to the desire to strengthen family relationships, according to a survey by PulteGroup. Builders may see an increase in demand for mother-in-law suites, dual-master suites, larger great rooms, and additional bathrooms.

Commercial Building Contractors

As evidenced by the overall growth of the domestic economy, the next few years portend modest growth for commercial building companies. Vertical IQ projects 4.33% compounded annual growth for commercial building contractors from 2017 to 2023, which is comparable to the growth of the overall economy (see Exhibit 2).

According to Vertical IQ, the following factors are influencing the growth in the commercial building market:

- *Construction growth improved*. Economic conditions have driven growth in the commercial construction market. The post-stimulus trough in federal spending resulted in stabilization of institutional projects, and the office building market has experienced

Exhibit 2. Commercial Building Contractors Industry Growth

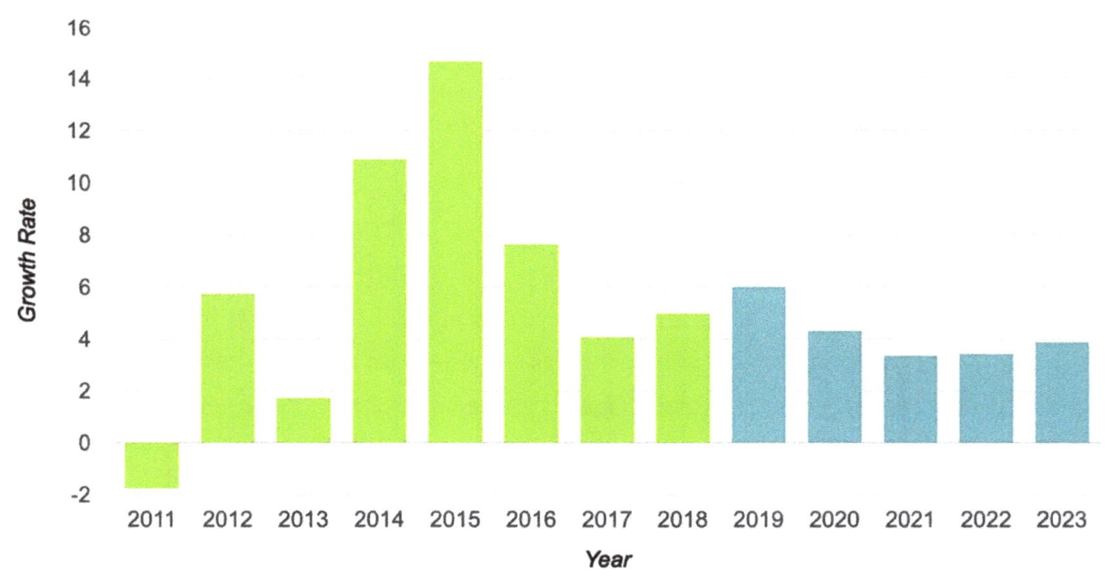

significant employment growth. Nonresidential construction spending grew by about 9% in 2014, 7% in 2015, and 4.8% in 2016. Spending slipped 0.5% in 2017 but returned to growth in 2018, rising 5.1% in the first 10 months of the year.

- *Financing available for key sectors.* While overall construction financing is still scarce, markets with better growth prospects have improved chances of obtaining credit. Projects in the healthcare, public works, education, state/local government, and institutional sectors are receiving funding due to market need or higher owner equity. As a result, competition for public-sector projects is increasing as more private-sector contractors attempt to diversify revenue streams. As reported by Dodge Analytics, institutional building will rise 3% in 2019, picking up the pace from a 1% gain in 2018 that followed an 18% gain in 2017. Educational facilities should see continued growth in 2019, supported by funding from numerous school construction bond measures. Healthcare projects will make a partial rebound after pulling back in 2018. Airport terminal and amusement-related projects are expected to stay close to the elevated levels of construction starts reported in 2017 and 2018. Further, public works construction will increase 4%. The omnibus federal appropriations bill passed in March 2018 provided greater funding for transportation projects that carried over into 2019, and environmental-related projects are getting a lift from recently passed legislation.

- *Corporate profit.* Corporate profit influences a business's ability to expand operations. As corporate profit rises, companies become more able and willing to open new locations and hire more workers, driving demand for new commercial construction. Corporate profit is expected to rise in 2020, according to the *Economic Outlook Update*.

As reported by Vertical IQ, the following trends will have an impact on the residential construction industry.

- *Green buildings.* Demand for environmentally friendly buildings continues to grow at a rapid pace. Presently, about 45% of all new commercial and institutional construction is considered green, up from 2% in 2005, according to the U.S. Green Building Council. Increased government regulation, market differentiation, growing awareness for LEED standards, and attractive financials are driving developers to implement more eco-friendly features. Green buildings typically have lower operating costs, higher values, and better ROIs than traditional buildings. Contractors that specialize in green construction can realize a distinct advantage.

- *Technology improves productivity.* Narrow margins and an increasingly competitive environment have led more contractors to implement technology that improves their productivity and enables them to provide cost estimates with greater accuracy. An increasing number of contractors are using Building Information Modeling (BIM) software, which integrates the design process with costing. BIM systems are dynamic and allow designers, contractors, and developers to access building information, make changes, and calculate the associated costs. Some programs link to estimating systems and generate work schedules for subcontractors as well as purchase orders for materials.

- *Office environments shrinking.* Although the past recession resulted in reduced demand for office space, the amount of square footage per worker has been shrinking for several decades. Space allocation per worker declined from 500 square feet in 1975 to about 200 square feet in 2010, according to Jones Lang LaSalle, but space increased slightly, to 240 square feet, in 2018. Younger workers have eschewed the traditional office layout in favor of communal spaces. Technology, such as laptops and cell phones, has also helped reduce space requirements. Many office tenants renewing leases have cut space. All of these factors could pose a threat to commercial building.

Construction Company Mergers and Acquisitions and ESOPs

Turning to buy-sell activity in the construction market, we saw a lot of merger and acquisition activity across North America in 2018, with over 400 closed or announced transactions. This is approximately a 33% increase from the number of deals closed or announced in 2017. The deals in 2018 were primarily defined by midsized or smaller strategic deals, which is much different than the larger, more-than-$1-billion deals we have seen in recent years.

Several factors have contributed to this active market, including activity from private equity firms, public companies looking for growth, and significant interest in specific sectors such as building and energy services. It should be noted, however, that a major driver of mergers and acquisition activity in the industry is also related to the demographic need for owner succession due to retiring baby boomers.

Along with traditional mergers and acquisitions, we're also seeing increased interest in employee stock option plans (ESOPs), which are discussed in Chapter 7, "Creating Value in a Construction Business," as an alternative exit strategy to selling a residential construction or commercial construction business. This change informs us that, as more owners evaluate their options, the tax-advantaged value creation afforded by an ESOP can be a great choice for many construction companies grappling with ownership transitions.

Summary

As discussed throughout this chapter, the market for both residential builders and commercial builders has been strong since 2012. In more recent years, we have seen a decline in growth, but one that is still generally within the expected growth in the economy as a whole. This decline, though, has business owners and investors wondering what the future will bring, especially as we see the future growth coming more in line with the overall growth for the U.S. economy. Are we heading into the next slowdown? Some say we are well overdue as the last slowdown was over a decade ago. The next chapter provides some insight into what to do going forward.

6. Are We Headed Toward the Next Downturn? What Can You Do

By Pasquale Rafanelli

Currently, the single most important question that business owners and investors should be asking themselves is where the market is headed. The current market climate for both residential builders and commercial builders has been strong since 2012. In more recent years, we have seen a decline in growth but one that is still in line with the expected growth in the U.S. economy as a whole. This decline has business owners and investors wondering what the future will bring. Are we heading into the next slowdown? Some say we are well overdue as the last slowdown was over a decade ago.

What does this mean for your future cash flows and more importantly for succession planning? A downturn could have a major impact on the value of your business, which could be a detriment or a benefit. For example, if you are looking to sell your business, the downturn could lower value, which would ultimately result in a lower purchase price. Of course, if you are trying to sell, this would not bode well with regard to a big payday. On the other hand, if you are looking to transfer your business to a family member through a gift, then this same downturn could lower the value of your business and result in a lower price. This is a major benefit because you can transfer your business at a reduced price and in turn use less of your lifetime exclusion and/or pay less gift tax.

If you are a business owner, now is the time to get proactive with conversations and planning, using lessons learned from the last downturn to recession-proof your company. While the last recession was historic in terms of scale and duration, the next downturn could potentially look very different. Still, through good preparation, companies can take the lessons they and their predecessors learned from the last recession and use them to avoid repeating any costly mistakes.

Below are some key lessons that all residential construction and commercial construction companies can learn from.

1. *Don't wait too long to make any hard decisions you have been deferring.* These tough decisions might take the form of letting go a marginal performer you've been keeping, cutting an underperforming office or division that has been limping along, or anything else you've been waiting to pull the trigger on. During the last recession, these types of issues plagued residential and commercial construction companies for far too long. Leadership that is slow to react and respond can make or break a company.

2. *Find your own sweet spot and don't just follow the herd.* Be picky and don't chase every project or competitor. Know what your core competencies are and with whom you like to work. Don't just be a market follower, especially if you are trailing behind others in markets where your company has little or no expertise. If you're following the crowd, you will be a year behind the latest movements.

3. *Work on the new and envisioned future and set the strategy for post-recession success.* Be clear on your organizational purpose and values during this exercise; they will be tested. Many of today's leaders are in constant firefighting mode and are not focused on the big picture. Living in a reactive mode and not being proactive can become your biggest detriment. Take charge of shaping your own destiny and future.

4. *Get a grasp on incremental economics such as revenue, margin, and overhead.* A good business doesn't turn on its head in a bad market. A competitive landscape has transformed standard estimating procedures into a game of marksmanship. Understanding the total costs for each project and how these costs break down is the first step in knowing where and how you can improve profit margins. Too many residential and commercial construction companies lack true knowledge of what it costs them to both perform the project and pursue new projects. In a recession, the ability to produce as inexpensively as possible is the key differentiator. If you know your historical costs, you can proactively reduce or raise your prices according to market conditions.

5. *Maintain a healthy balance sheet (i.e., cash and working capital) in the context of growth plans.* Conduct a risk analysis on all existing projects slated to complete more than six

months out. Identify high-risk projects and how each will be staffed to take the project to completion. Leverage and utilize a multiskilled workforce: In-house self-performing capabilities can make a big difference on margins, time, and workforce capacity, while all-around adaptability can make a firm indispensable to satisfied clients.

6. *Get positioned early in your market as a thought leader.* The game of selling work and interacting with clients has changed quite a bit for many residential and commercial construction companies. These days, early plans allow for the most flexibility. Look closely at segments that are likely to do well in a recession. Are you winning the size and type of work that will allow you to quickly expand in the event of a market change? Do you truly understand your clients' mindsets? Do you get their way of thinking and what's important to them? While client relationships won't guarantee you work, they do still matter and are critical when the market slows down.

7. *Get more feet on the street.* It's time to give your salespeople the skills they need to be confident calling on customers. Have them build a list of contacts that they want to keep in touch with. Then, create a training program to educate your staff on how to manage the company in a recession. Interaction across all company levels will increase their presence in the market and give them an inside track to improve collaboration among future leaders.

This year and beyond, we can expect to see buyers be more cautious with their acquisition activity. Not that we expect the activity will cease, but firms will probably be more selective about where they place their bets given where we are in the current economic cycle.

At the start of the last recession, contractors had large backlogs, and many thought they would weather the storm. In reality, almost all of that backlog disappeared relatively quickly. At first, it was deferred, then it was postponed, and then it was gone all together. It may not happen this way next time, but, if we learned anything, history could repeat itself. Today, a lot of work is being delayed and schedules are constantly slowed. Perhaps this is a precursor to the next slowdown, and, in any case, it is a major red flag that we should all keep an eye on as we proceed through 2020 and 2021.

SECTION III:

SELLING AND SUCCESSION PLANNING OF A RESIDENTIAL/NONRESIDENTIAL CONSTRUCTION COMPANY

7. Creating Value in a Construction Business

By Pasquale Rafanelli

Creating value and goodwill above the value derived from accumulated earnings requires much more than just making money. It requires building an organization that makes money with or without the owner.

Value creation is a rational goal of any business owner. Eventually, when the time comes for the business owner to sell, the potential buyer's assessment of the value created may not coincide with the seller's assessment of what the business is worth. Human nature can explain some of the differences between the seller's and buyer's opinions of value. However, in the construction industry, many of the differences can often be found in how the business owner went about creating value in his or her business.

How Value is Created in a Construction Business

A business owner can create value in the following three ways:

1. Accumulation of earnings;
2. Growth in earnings; and
3. Creation of goodwill.

Accumulation of earnings. Using the accumulation of earnings method, the business owner makes as much money as possible but without creating an enterprise that is salable for more than its asset value. Hence, the appraiser uses the asset approach to value the business and applies all or most of the weight in his or her conclusion of value to this approach, which, in most cases, is the floor value.

Most construction companies, particularly smaller firms, fall into the accumulation of earnings category. The owner's goal is to make money and realize the firm's earnings by distributing earnings. They eventually sell the business for its adjusted book value. This is done either through an earnout based on future earnings or by liquidating the company. In this scenario, goodwill is not created, and the business does not have a value that is separate from the assets and liabilities it accumulates.

Growth in earnings. Alternatively, using the growth in earnings method, the business owner creates the business so that its value is tied to its earnings capacity. This is done knowing that a buyer will eventually pay some multiple of earnings for the business.

A company that uses the growth in earnings method is typically worth a multiple of its earnings. A general rule of thumb is a multiple of three to five times its pretax earnings. Through various business strategies, the earnings are grown and then the increased earnings are multiplied by the appropriate multiple. Therefore, the increase in earnings, not an increase in multiple, creates the value.

Creation of goodwill. The creation of goodwill method includes the growth in earnings method. Goodwill is the value of a business above its asset value, and it is created in various ways including building a solid customer list, having good customer relationships, creating employee trust, having a trusted brand name, and more. The creation of goodwill method is defined as creating value by making the unsalable company salable. In essence, this method makes a company that would sell for book or asset value sell for a premium or makes a company that sells for a multiple of earnings sell for a higher multiple.

Not many construction companies create goodwill. Empirical statistics cited for companies of all sizes in the construction industry show that approximately 30% will eventually liquidate, approximately 60% will sell or transfer to family or employees, and approximately 10% will eventually sell to a third party.

Companies that liquidate create value by accumulating earnings. Companies that sell or transfer to family or employees mostly create value for their owner by accumulating earnings, though some may realize a premium. Sales to a third party could be at asset value or greater and could use any of the three methods described above.

The implication of the statistics cited above is that not many construction companies create goodwill—though most accumulate earnings. The reason behind this may have something to do with the fragmentation of the construction industry. This industry is fragmented because:

- Most building markets are local; and
- There are limited economies of scale.

Limitations and Risks to the Creation of Value

Several factors influence the creation of value for a construction company. Some of the most prominent factors are covered below.

Purchasing advantages. Purchasing advantages for construction companies vary widely, as suppliers often support the local business to avoid being too dependent on the national or regional business.

Fragmentation. The effect of fragmentation on the construction industry is that the locally owned and managed businesses often outcompete national or regional firms a division manager runs.

Cyclical business. What is built over time is cyclical. Market opportunities typically come in waves, and five years is an eternity in the construction industry. Successful firms are able to move fast with the waves of construction activity and are flexible enough to grow smaller or larger when needed. A locally owned and managed business often has the flexibility needed to compete against larger national or regional firms.

Economic factors. Businesses often struggle in economic downturns because of reduced margins. In addition, banks and sureties that are often supportive in good economic markets turn away from construction firms in down markets.

The construction industry typically enters into a 10-year cycle, and, approximately every 10 years, something happens—often external to the construction industry—that negatively affects the construction markets. Some examples include:

- The oil embargo in the 1970s;
- Interest rates peaking at more than 20% in the 1980s;
- The savings and loan crisis of the 1990s;
- The World Trade Center attack and bank collapses in the 2000s; and
- The housing market crash in 2008.

Each of these events caused dramatic downturns in the construction industry, often confounding the best efforts of industry entrepreneurs in value creation and consolidation.

All of these factors make value creation, beyond accumulation of earnings, difficult for a construction firm. Growth by diversifying into another business's geographic market creates added competition with locally owned businesses. Growth by diversifying into a new type of construction runs the risk of getting into the market at the wrong time and facing competition in an unfamiliar market. Investing in an acquisition strategy to consolidate a market runs the risks of the market declining, struggling to integrate an acquired company, paying too much to an unmotivated seller, or paying too much to a seller in the midst of an industry consolidation wave.

How to Create Goodwill

Owners of private companies often acknowledge the difficulty in creating goodwill in their buy-sell, operating, or stockholder agreements by using book value or some form of book value for their valuation. This may be a deliberate avoidance to include any goodwill in the business valuation, or it may represent conservatism or just a desire to keep the valuation methodology simple by using the results of the balance sheet the accountant or valuation analyst prepared.

With this thinking as a backdrop, how does a construction firm create goodwill (i.e., a business that a buyer will purchase at a value beyond its assets and accumulated earnings value)? The drivers that create goodwill in this industry are covered as follows.

A leadership culture. A construction firm is a group of people who are employed, perform, and are paid for the projects and services they provide. If you were to remove the people, then all you have are the business's assets and liabilities. A leadership culture is one that develops exceptional people. The result of a good leadership culture is that can grow by expanding the organization.

An ability to find and exploit opportunities. The slow growth and cyclical construction market is made up of numerous construction markets that cycle with intensity. Profit margins in various sectors tend to vary widely. The value-creating firm is able to quickly find and move to new and profitable opportunities, which help it grow and prosper.

Financial discipline. An interesting article from *Construction Executive Magazine*,[1] found that, while the nature of the industry and the economy are contributing factors to failure, the primary reasons are poor strategic decisions or lack of financial discipline that lead to capital erosion. Bad things will happen to businesses in this industry, and there is no substitute for a strong balance sheet and the financial discipline to enable a business to go after the next set of opportunities.

Taken together, the following three drivers can create value in the buyer's mind:

1. Provide the potential buyer with the confidence that there will be the best leaders and organization to facilitate growth. This is in contrast to many businesses where the selling owner is the sole driving force in the business.

2. Provide the potential buyer with the confidence that the business will be able to enter and exit markets when the company's current market cycles end. This is in contrast to a business that has been successful only in a single service, market sector, or geographic market.

3. Provide the potential buyer with the confidence that the business has financial systems and controls in place to identify problems and opportunities early and the decision-making skills to react appropriately.

Ownership structure for value creation. Realizing goodwill in the value of a business also requires adopting an ownership structure to exploit opportunity. There are five typical ownership structures:

1 *Construction Executive Magazine,* Sept. 2, 2014 (obtained at constructionexec.com/article/why-contractors-fail on May 23, 2019).

1. *Private structure.* This is the least likely structure to result in payment for goodwill. In fact, goodwill in a valuation for a business's private ownership structure may work against the survival of the business as a private firm because, if the stock price is too high, a sale to employees or back to the company may put financial strain on the business, leading to a loss of financial discipline and capacity. The other four ownership structures covered below all offer the opportunity for a valuation and sale of stock at a value that includes goodwill.

2. *Private equity.* Private equity is a pool of funds investors provide that a management firm manages and invests. The investors in private equity typically include high-net-worth individuals, endowments, and pension funds. There are thousands of private equity funds investing pools of money in all types of businesses. A segment of these funds invest in engineering and construction firms.

   Private equity provides two opportunities for a seller to realize value from its business. First, if a business meets its investment criteria, the private equity fund will pay a multiple of earnings or cash flow for a portion of the business. Typically, it will not buy 100% of a business. However, if this occurs, private equity managers will then encourage and possibly help the business increase its value by increasing earnings, which makes the business more salable.

   Another opportunity for the seller is to realize that value can be derived from a second sale—typically three to seven years after the first purchase—wherein both the current private equity fund and the participating managers realize capital gains. Private equity is very selective about where it will invest. It likely will pay for goodwill in a purchase, and its hope and intent are to dramatically increase the goodwill realized in the second sale.

3. *Strategic sale.* In a strategic sale, a business sells to a third-party buyer, such as a larger private company, public company, or a private-equity-backed company. The profitability of the business, its asset base, as well as intangible and strategic factors drive value. Buyers have their own motives and interests for an acquisition, and this will drive their perception of value. Strategic purchasers may seek to enter new markets, consolidate a market, build out a national footprint, or have a host of other strategic intentions. Ultimately, value is negotiated between buyer and seller based on both parties' interests and motives.

4. *Public IPO/SPAC.* An initial public offering (IPO) is a process whereby a business can sell a portion of its stock to the public. The public, as defined here, includes institutional and individual investors. After the IPO, the business's stock trades on an exchange. The business's underlying fundamentals, industry and market trends, and comparable stocks within the same industry drive value.

5. *Employee stock ownership plan (ESOP).* This is an employee-owner program that provides a company's workforce with an ownership interest in the company. In an ESOP, companies provide their employees with stock ownership, often at no upfront cost to the employees. ESOP shares, however, are part of employees' remuneration for work performed. Shares are allocated to employees and may be held in an ESOP trust until the employee retires or leaves the company. The shares are then either bought back by the company for redistribution or voided.

Pitfalls in the Construction Industry

Many of the characteristics that are unique to the construction industry are key contributors to a contractor's financial difficulties. The following is a discussion of some of these factors.

Leverage. In the construction industry, "leverage" is leveraging working capital or leveraging equity. High leverage for contractors typically refers to the amount of revenue pushed through the pipeline compared to the underlying equity base or level of working capital. Contractors, especially those in the building market, can do a large amount of business with a little bit of equity.

Workforce issues. The construction industry is a people business, and, without the right people in the right places, contractors are bound to get into trouble. Where will these people come from, and where will a construction firm find technically qualified people to do the work in the pipeline now and in the future?

The cyclical nature of the industry. Construction activity rises and falls faster than the overall economy. Such fluctuations lead to being overcommitted or scrambling for work to keep people busy. Both of these scenarios can lead to problems.

The hard-bid process. Work is procured in a large part of the construction industry differently than it is for other businesses. The owner wants a building and wants to know exactly how much it will cost before the project is built. Increasing complexity of projects and fluctuating materials costs and labor concerns all conspire to make this a dangerous get-work practice for contractors. While the predominance of this method is changing with new delivery methods, it is easy to see how contractors still get into trouble here.

Project timing. Dictated by owners' schedules, contractors have little control over project start dates. Sometimes project opportunities become available at the same time, leading to overcommitment of company resources. In other cases, project start dates slip, creating staffing and financing challenges for the contractor. Backlogs can fluctuate widely. A related issue is long project durations, which can result in project impacts due to material, labor, weather, and related issues.

Derived demand. Most businesses think they have the ability to affect the demand for their service or product. If a company wants more business, then it conducts more marketing to create the demand for its product or service. On the other hand, contractors are always responding to opportunities. Ninety-nine percent of the work done in the construction industry comes from contractors responding to available work. Therefore, contractors are at the mercy of the work that comes their way.

The hypercompetitive construction industry. Construction is an easy business to get into. Low barriers to entry and price-driven competition lead to a very competitive industry. In addition, when every project is unique, contractors don't get to practice. The learning curve can be expensive, and not all learning is portable to the next project.

Conclusion

Opening up your business to the market is the ultimate test for the creation of goodwill. However, many owners do not test the market to see whether a buyer will recognize their value, as they prefer to remain independent. Toward the end of their careers, many engineering and construction business owners are disappointed when they discover that the value of their business is tied more to its asset value or a nominal multiple of earnings than to any goodwill they assumed had been created. It is often difficult to explain to these owners that their notion of goodwill does not hold in a buyer's mind because the goodwill is overly dependent upon the selling owner as a person. In addition, the buyer could potentially see risk where the owner potentially sees opportunity, and, therefore, the buyer's perception of value is tempered.

Creating value and goodwill above accumulated earnings requires more than making money. As covered throughout this chapter, it requires building an organization that makes money with or without the owner. It requires a corporate culture that is continuously developing people to expand the capabilities of the organization. It requires a corporate culture that is forever in search of new opportunities in the industry and one that has the ability to take advantage of those opportunities. The organizations that can build a culture of developing their people and create processes to constantly identify and exploit new opportunities are those that are most likely to create value and goodwill.

8. Succession Planning Builds Construction Company Value

By Pasquale Rafanelli

Business value is dependent upon the predictability that earnings will continue after a transfer of ownership occurs, whether by sale, gift, or estate bequest. One of the most important points of having a succession plan is to build the present value of the business to pass on to and through the next generation.

Succession planning will give you the peace of mind that your heirs will not trip and fall after the transfer of control, that the business partners can make good on the installment note to purchase your stock, or put more cash in your pocket when you sell the business.

As we've discussed earlier in this special report, succession planning is especially critical for the value of construction companies for a few reasons. First, these are often family-run businesses started by a sole owner and can become overreliant on the goodwill of the owner. As a result, absent a succession plan, it can be hard to ensure there is real value to the business once the principal owner is no longer involved.

Second, in some instances of construction companies with a unionized workforce, succession planning can help with a better understanding of any pension liabilities that may become relevant during an ownership transfer.

Most importantly, as the founder contemplates exiting the business, either through sale or transfer to family members, a succession plan positions the founder to best realize the financial gains that should come from the growth of the business and its client base.

Loyd Rawls, founder and CEO of the Rawls Group, says firm owners can start their succession planning by asking themselves the following four questions.

1. *What is your motivation?* Why did you start the business and what do you want to accomplish with it? If you don't have a vision for where you want to end up, creating a plan to get there will be next to impossible. There is a slim chance that everything will fall into place and things will all happen at the exact right time. Leaving your business's future in the hands of luck is much more likely to produce a tragedy rather than a legacy.

2. *How financially independent are you from your business?* Make sure you've done enough personal estate planning to have the liquidity that will allow you to pull out of the business when you're ready. To remain in full control of your destiny, make sure you are financially independent from the business, so it is your personal choice to continue to work versus it being a matter of necessity.

3. *How is the business performing?* You will need a heightened level of business performance to successfully navigate the transition to new leadership. As the successor will inevitably make some less-than-perfect decisions, the business needs to be strong enough to withstand them. Having extra capital in reserve for these situations will help the successor learn without jeopardizing the business's future. Other important business performance areas that should be performing above average include employee turnover rates, market penetration, and customer satisfaction. Maintaining excellent vendor relationships and introducing your successor to your vendors will allow them to develop solid relationships before your departure will be vital as well. Because so much of the construction business is rooted in goodwill, this is also an opportunity to strategize a way to realize the full value of the business by ensuring the successor is best positioned to continue those relationships—especially when the success of the business could be dependent on just a handful of these relationships.

Remember that the new successor's "hiccups" are necessary to his or her development and should not be viewed as a sign that he or she is incapable. Rather, these bumps in the road simply show that your successor is human and will learn from his or her mistakes like everyone else does in life.

4. *Have you identified and developed a successor?* How is your management synergy and teamwork? Identifying your successor requires a lot more than selecting a person and putting his or her name down on a piece of paper. To have a capable and committed successor be ready to take over the reins, he or she must be developed.

It is critical that the current leaders coach and mentor the successor on business operations and management and leadership skills. Those who are named successors should start from the ground up and know every aspect of the business and be thoroughly integrated into client relationships. If you allow them to take the elevator to upper management rather than the stairs, they will miss the opportunity to earn the respect of fellow employees and managers who they will one day be leading.

SECTION IV:
RESIDENTIAL/NONRESIDENTIAL CONSTRUCTION COMPANY BENCHMARKING DATA AND RESEARCH

9. Residential Builder Valuation Multiples Based on DealStats[1]

By Adam Manson

To determine the value of a residential builder business, it is important to know the price at which similar businesses have been sold. Business appraisers often apply the selling price multiples from comparable companies that they find in transaction databases, such as DealStats, to their subject company's underlying financial data to develop an indication of value. These data points are also helpful to the business owner when benchmarking the value of his or her business.

This chapter presents data from DealStats on residential builders that sold between 1996 and 2019. The analysis includes 126 residential builder purchases from a population of 37,462 business purchases across all industries. The data presented include medians, the middle number in an ordered set, and averages. A selling price-to-revenue ratio (also known as a valuation multiple) of 0.30, for example, translates to a residential building company that sold for 30% of its last 12 months of revenues.

Of the 126 transactions, 116 provide information on company type: 50% of residential builders are S corporations, 15.5% are C corporations, 25% are LLCs, 4.3% are sole proprietorships,

1 DealStats, available at bvresources.com/DealStats, is a robust online database boasting the most complete financial details on thousands of acquired private companies, with nearly 200 data points per sale. With six valuation multiples and 13 financial ratios, each transaction includes detailed data vital to applying the market approach, deriving a selling price, benchmarking performance, or performing a fairness opinion analysis. The detailed, transaction-by-transaction data used for this chapter can be purchased at bvresources.com/DealStats by searching SIC codes 1521 and 1522.

and 5.2% are classified as "Other" (see Exhibit 1). When compared to other industries, residential builders are more likely to operate as an S corporation (50% versus 44.5%) and less likely to operate as a sole proprietorship (4.3% versus 8.7%).

Of the residential builder transactions from DealStats that reported sale type, 87.3% are asset deals and 12.7% are stock deals. This compares to 78.7% asset type and 21.3% stock type for all other businesses (see Exhibit 2).

Residential builder selling price multiples. As shown in Exhibit 3, the median selling price multiple for residential builder company transactions is 0.3 times revenues, 2.1 times seller's discretionary earnings (SDE), and 3.0 times earnings before interest, taxes, depreciation, and amortization (EBITDA).

Exhibit 1. Residential Builders—Company Types

	Count	% of Total
S corporation	58	50.0%
Sole proprietorship	5	4.3%
LLC	29	25.0%
C corporation	18	15.5%
Other	6	5.2%

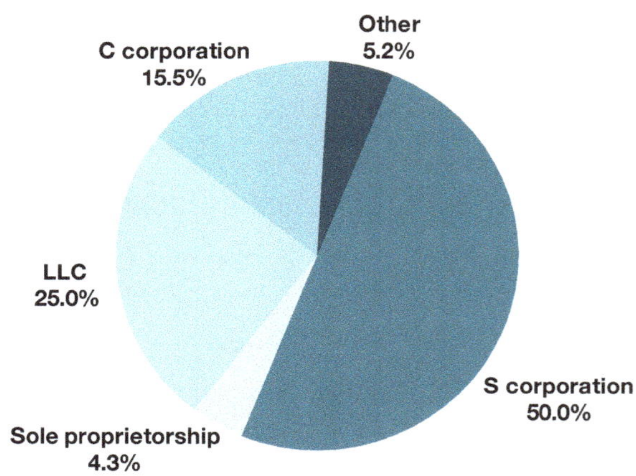

Exhibit 2. Residential Builders—Sale Type

	Count	% of Total
Asset	110	87.3%
Stock	16	12.7%

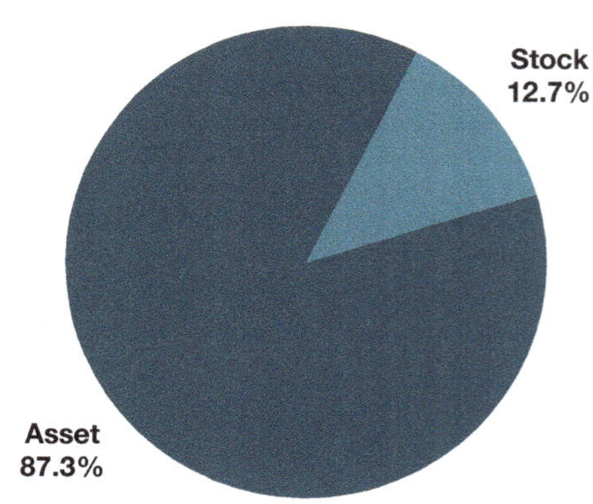

Residential builders compared to all businesses. When compared to all other businesses, the median selling price for residential builders based on revenue is lower than the median selling price for all other businesses (0.3 versus 0.5), as shown in Exhibit 4. The median selling price based on SDE is also lower (2.1 versus 2.5). The median selling price based on EBITDA for residential builders is 3.0, compared to 4.2 for all other businesses.

Exhibit 3. Residential Builder Company Selling Price Multiples

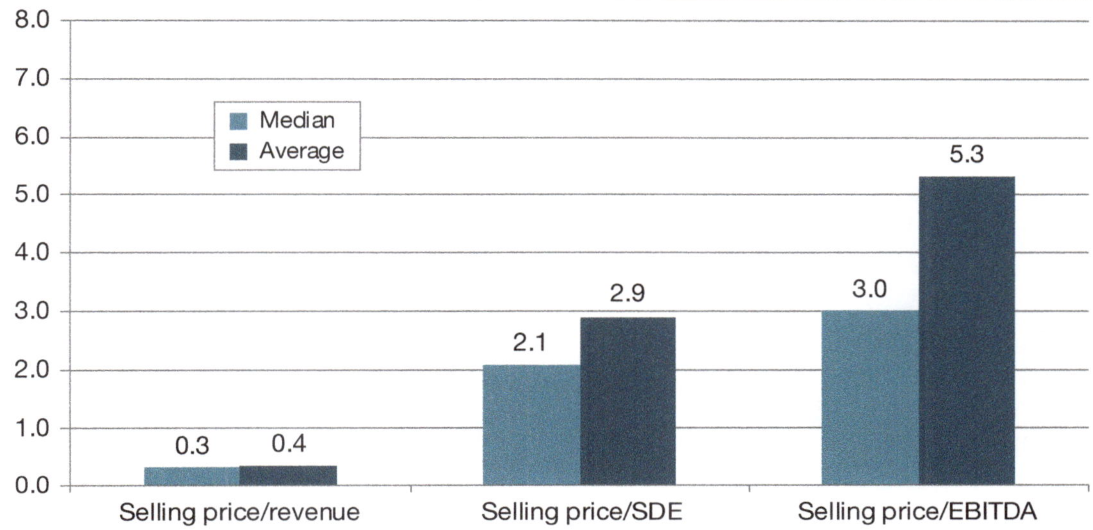

SDE = seller's discretionary earnings
EBITDA = earnings before interest, taxes, depreciation, and amortization
Values over 100 have been eliminated.

Exhibit 4. Median Selling Price Multiples

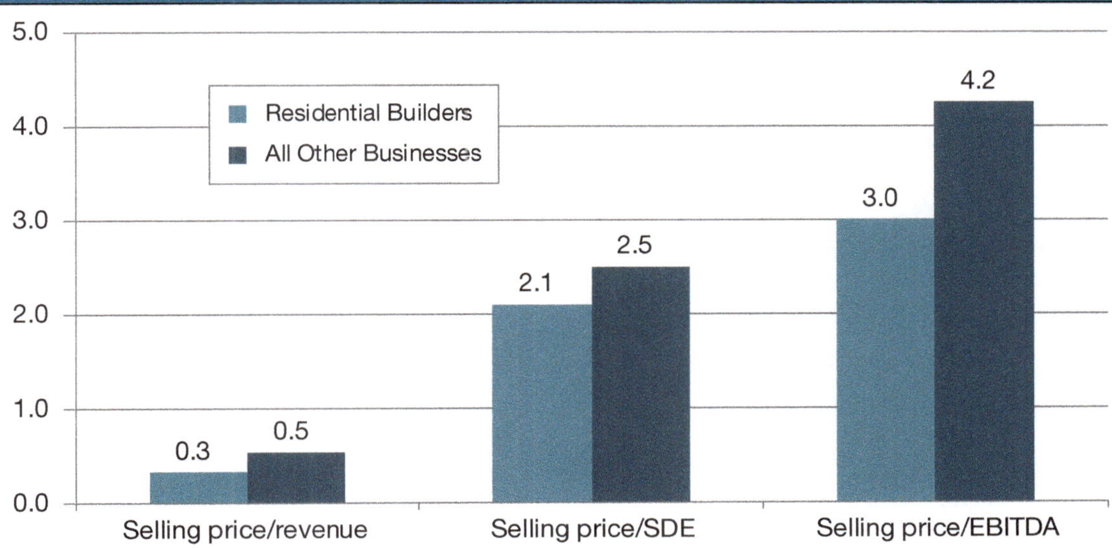

SDE = seller's discretionary earnings
EBITDA = earnings before interest, taxes, depreciation, and amortization
Values over 100 have been eliminated.

Average selling price multiples. When comparing the average selling price multiples of residential builders versus all other businesses, residential builders fare worse than other businesses in relation to selling price based on revenue (0.4 versus 1.3), SDE (2.9 versus 3.5), and EBITDA (5.3 versus 8.3). See Exhibit 5.

Exhibit 5. Average Selling Price Multiples

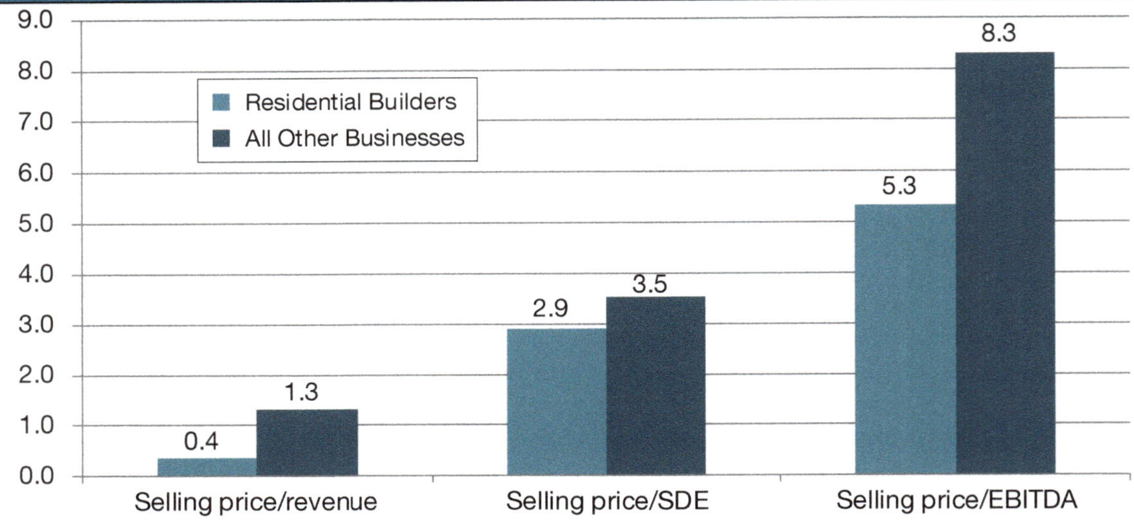

SDE = seller's discretionary earnings
EBITDA = earnings before interest, taxes, depreciation, and amortization
Values over 100 have been eliminated.

Exhibit 6. Median Profit Margins

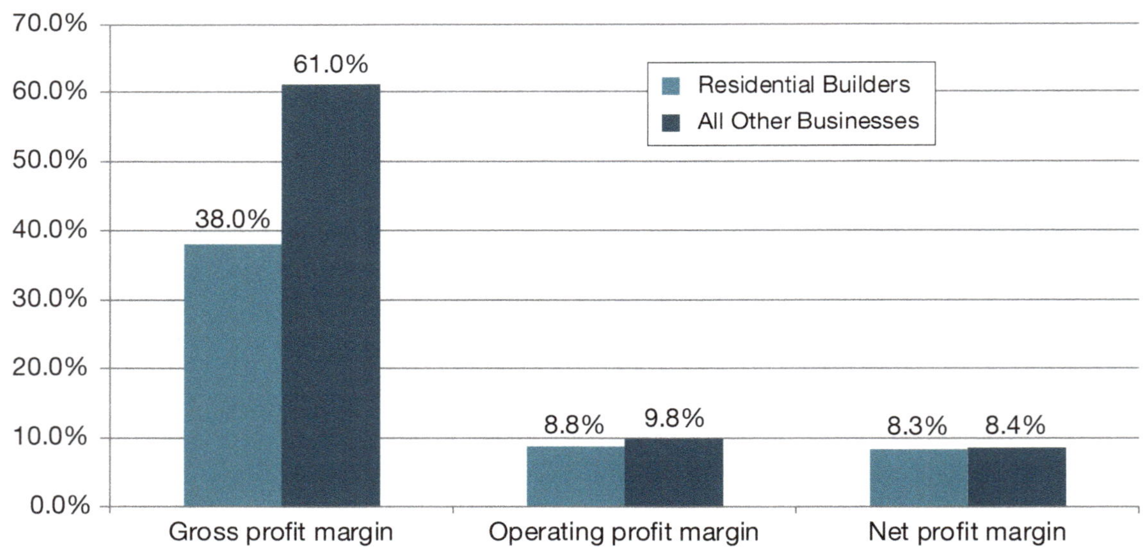

Gross profit margin = gross profit/revenue
Operating profit margin = operating profit/revenue
Net profit margin = net income/revenue

Profit margins. Residential builders have lower median profit margins than other businesses, according to data from DealStats. The gross profit margin for residential builders is 38%, compared to 61% for all other businesses. The operating profit margin for residential builders is 8.8%, compared to 9.8% for all other businesses, and the net profit margin for residential builders is 8.3%, compared to 8.4% for all other businesses (see Exhibit 6).

Exhibits 7, 8, and 9 display the interquartile range of selling prices of residential builders relative to other businesses. The interquartile range provides a measure of dispersion. Interquartile range is the difference between the 25th and 75th percentiles (also called the first and third quartiles), so the interquartile range describes the middle 50% of observations. The top of the orange rectangle indicates the 75th percentile, the bottom of the blue rectangle indicates the 25th percentile, and the line where the two rectangles meet represents the median. If the interquartile range is large, it means the middle 50% of observations are spaced far apart, and, if the interquartile range is narrow, it means the middle 50% of observations are spaced close together.

Exhibit 7. Selling Price/Revenue—Interquartile Range

	Residential Builders	All Other Businesses
90th percentile	0.7	2.0
75th percentile	0.5	0.9
Median	0.3	0.5
25th percentile	0.2	0.3
10th percentile	0.1	0.2

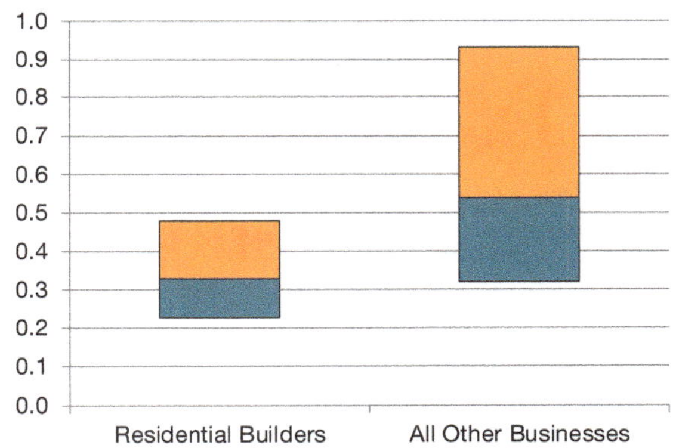

The graph displays the interquartile range. The blue rectangle indicates the spread between the first quartile (or 25th percentile) and the median, and the orange rectangle indicates the spread between the median and the third quartile (or 75th percentile).

Values over 100 have been eliminated.

Exhibit 8. Selling Price/SDE—Interquartile Range

	Residential Builders	All Other Businesses
90th percentile	4.3	5.8
75th percentile	3.1	3.6
Median	2.1	2.5
25th percentile	1.3	1.6
10th percentile	0.9	1.1

The graph displays the interquartile range. The blue rectangle indicates the spread between the first quartile (or 25th percentile) and the median, and the orange rectangle indicates the spread between the median and the third quartile (or 75th percentile).

SDE = seller's discretionary earnings
Values over 100 have been eliminated.

Operating and net profit margins are provided in Exhibits 10 and 11. The profit margins are plotted on the graphs by percentiles for both. The blue line represents the profit margins for residential builders, while the red line represents all other businesses. The median (or the 50th percentile) is where the lines intersect and 50% of the observations have a higher value and

Exhibit 9. Selling Price/EBITDA—Interquartile Range

	Residential Builders	All Other Businesses
90th percentile	11.0	18.2
75th percentile	6.4	8.9
Median	3.0	4.2
25th percentile	1.9	2.2
10th percentile	1.2	1.3

The graph displays the interquartile range. The blue rectangle indicates the spread between the first quartile (or 25th percentile) and the median, and the orange rectangle indicates the spread between the median and the third quartile (or 75th percentile).

EBITDA = earnings before interest, taxes, depreciation, and amortization
Values over 100 have been eliminated.

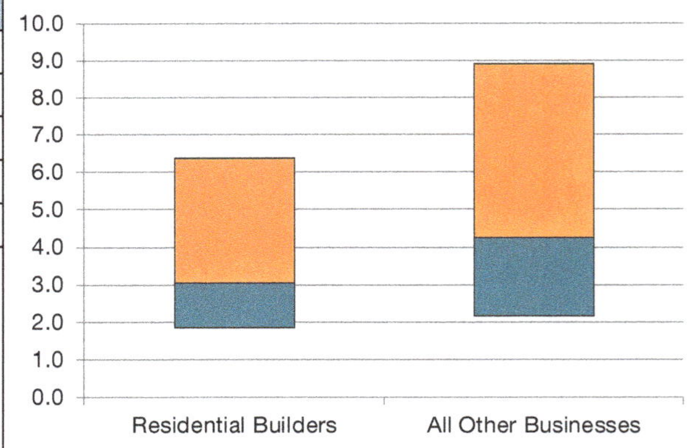

Exhibit 10. Operating Profit Margin—Interquartile Range

	Residential Builders	All Other Businesses
90th percentile	25.1%	35.3%
75th percentile	15.2%	21.2%
Median	8.8%	9.8%
25th percentile	3.7%	1.9%
10th percentile	0.6%	-6.4%

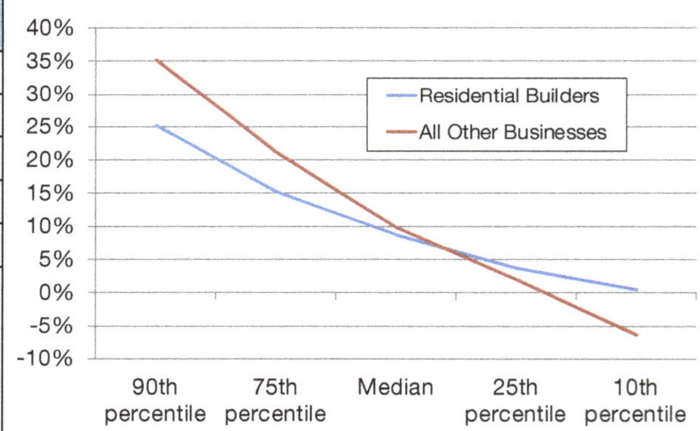

Exhibit 11. Net Profit Margin—Interquartile Range

	Residential Builders	All Other Businesses
90th percentile	24.4%	34.1%
75th percentile	15.3%	19.9%
Median	8.3%	8.4%
25th percentile	3.3%	1.0%
10th percentile	0.1%	-8.0%

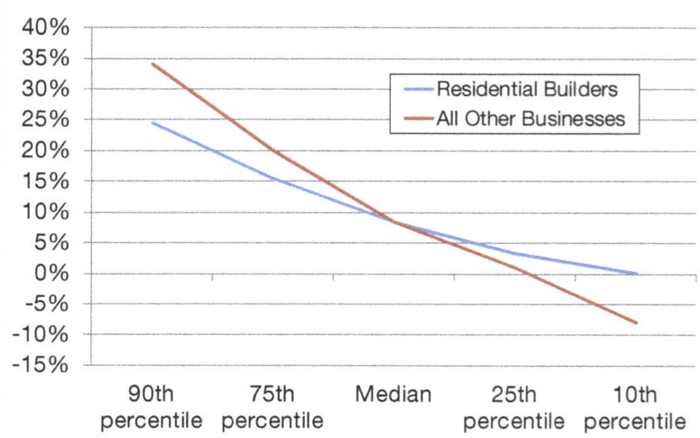

50% of the observations have a lower value. When reviewing the graphs, we see that the spread between the 10th percentile and the 90th percentile is less for residential builders relative to all other businesses, so it appears there is less variability in profits for residential builders relative to other businesses.

The median operating profit margin for residential builders is 8.8%, lower than the 9.8% operating profit margin for other businesses.

The median net profit margin for residential builders is 8.3%, compared with 8.4% for other businesses.

Median ratios. Median ratios are provided in Exhibit 12. The quick ratio measures a company's ability to meet its short-term obligations with its most liquid assets. The data indicate that residential builders have a quick ratio similar to other businesses in DealStats and therefore similar liquidity (both 1.1). The return on equity ratio measures a business's profitability by displaying how much profit a company generates with the money shareholders have invested. The data indicate that residential builders generate higher profits from equity investments than do other businesses (0.59 versus 0.25). The fixed-asset turnover ratio measures a business's ability to generate net sales from fixed-asset investments (specifically property, plant, and equipment, net of depreciation). Residential builders generate almost triple the sales relative to fixed assets when compared to other businesses (30.6 versus 10.8).

Exhibit 12. Median Ratios

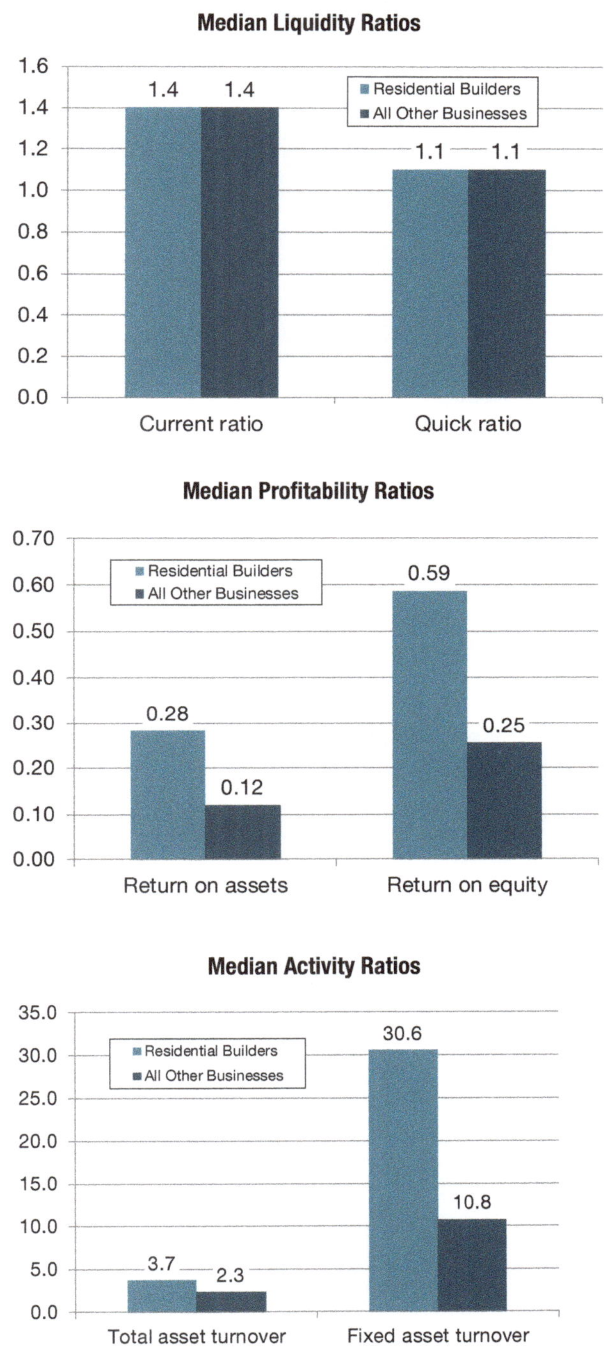

Current ratio = current assets/current liabilities
Quick ratio = (current assets - inventory)/current liabilities
Total asset turnover = revenue/total assets
Fixed asset turnover = revenue/fixed assets
Return on assets = net income/total assets
Return on equity = net income/equity

10. Nonresidential Builder Valuation Multiples Based on DealStats[1]

By Adam Manson

To determine the value of a nonresidential builder business, it is important to know the price at which similar businesses have been sold. Business appraisers often apply the selling price multiples from comparable companies that they find in transaction databases, such as DealStats, to their subject company's underlying financial data to develop an indication of value. These data points are also helpful to the business owner when benchmarking the value of his or her business.

This chapter presents data from DealStats on nonresidential builders that sold between 1999 and 2017.[2] The analysis includes 26 nonresidential builder purchases from a population of 37,462 business purchases across all industries. The data presented include medians, the middle number in an ordered set, and averages. A selling price-to-revenue ratio (also known as a valuation multiple) of 0.30, for example, translates to a nonresidential building company that sold for 30% of its last 12 months of revenues.

Of the 26 transactions, 24 provide information on company type: 75% of nonresidential builders are S corporations, 20.8% are C corporations, 4.2% are LLCs, 0% are sole proprietorships,

1 DealStats, available at bvresources.com/DealStats, is a robust online database boasting the most complete financial details on thousands of acquired private companies, with nearly 200 data points per sale. With six valuation multiples and 13 financial ratios, each transaction includes detailed data vital to applying the market approach, deriving a selling price, benchmarking performance, or performing a fairness opinion analysis. The detailed, transaction-by-transaction data used for this chapter can be purchased at bvresources.com/DealStats by searching SIC codes 1541 and 1542.

2 This is the most recent date for which the sale of a nonresidential building company was reported in DealStats.

and 0% are classified as "Other" (see Exhibit 1). When compared to other industries, nonresidential builders are more likely to operate as an S corporation (75% versus 44.5%) and less likely to operate as a sole proprietorship (0% versus 8.7%).

Of the 26 nonresidential builder transactions from DealStats, 57.7% are asset deals and 42.3% are stock deals. This compares to 78.7% asset type and 21.3% stock type deals for all other businesses (see Exhibit 2).

Nonresidential builder selling price multiples. As shown in Exhibit 3, the median selling price multiple for nonresidential builder company transactions is 0.4 times revenues, 2.7 times seller's discretionary earnings (SDE), and 4.3 times earnings before interest, taxes, depreciation, and amortization (EBITDA).

Exhibit 1. Nonresidential Builders—Company Types

	Count	% of Total
S corporation	18	75.0%
Sole proprietorship	0	0.0%
LLC	1	4.2%
C corporation	5	20.8%
Other	0	0.0%

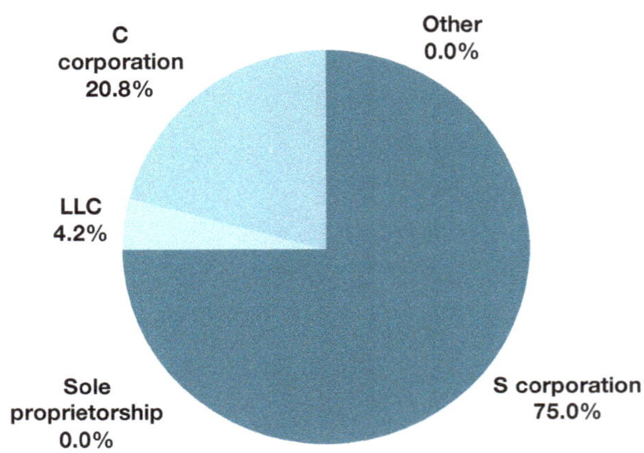

Exhibit 2. Nonresidential Builders—Sale Type

	Count	% of Total
Asset	15	57.7%
Stock	11	42.3%

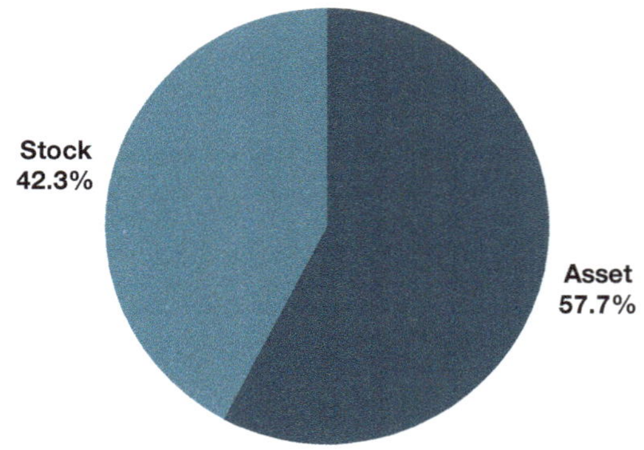

Nonresidential builders compared to all businesses. When compared to all other businesses, the median selling price for nonresidential builders based on revenue is lower than the median selling price for all other businesses (0.4 versus 0.5), as shown in Exhibit 4. The median selling price based on SDE is higher (2.7 versus 2.5). The median selling price based on EBITDA for nonresidential builders is 4.3, compared to 4.2 for all other businesses.

Exhibit 3. Nonresidential Builder Company Selling Price Multiples

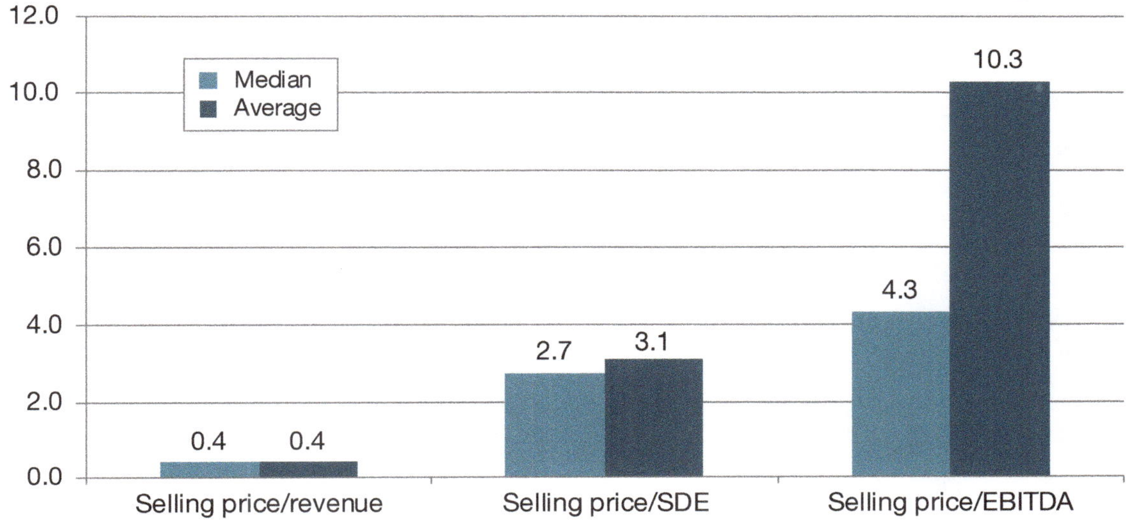

SDE = seller's discretionary earnings
EBITDA = earnings before interest, taxes, depreciation, and amortization
Values over 100 have been eliminated.

Exhibit 4. Median Selling Price Multiples

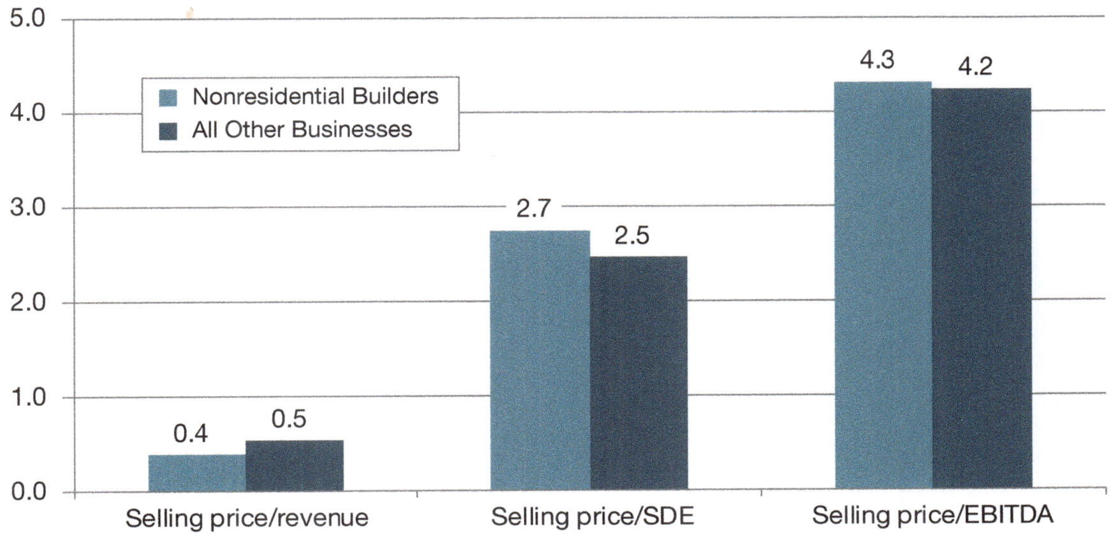

SDE = seller's discretionary earnings
EBITDA = earnings before interest, taxes, depreciation, and amortization
Values over 100 have been eliminated.

Average selling price multiples. When comparing the average selling price multiples of nonresidential builders to all other businesses, nonresidential builders fare worse in relation to selling price based on revenue (0.4 versus 1.3) and SDE (3.1 versus 3.5). However, they fare better than other businesses in relation to EBITDA (10.3 versus 8.3). See Exhibit 5.

Exhibit 5. Average Selling Price Multiples

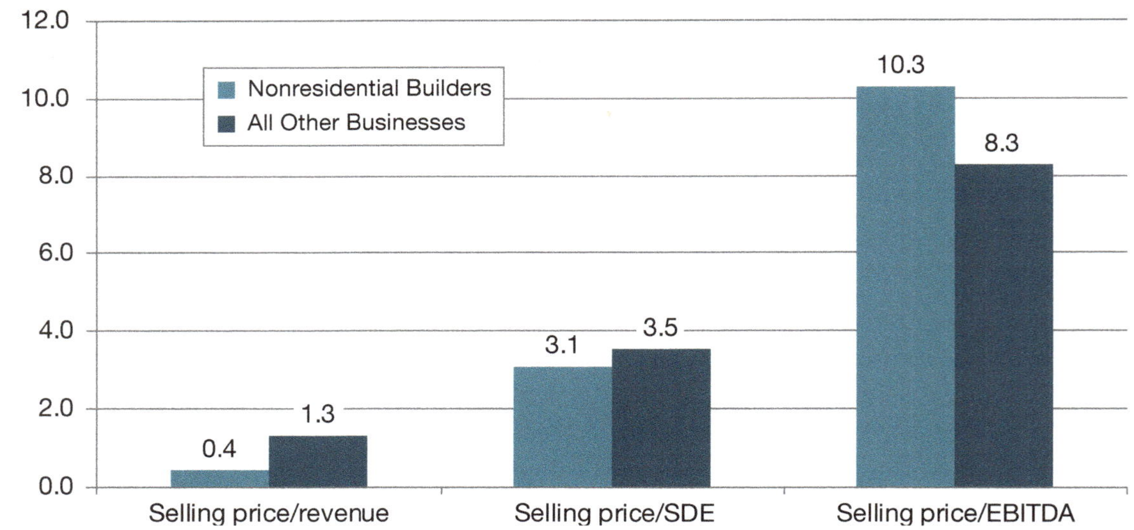

SDE = seller's discretionary earnings
EBITDA = earnings before interest, taxes, depreciation, and amortization
Values over 100 have been eliminated.

Exhibit 6. Median Profit Margins

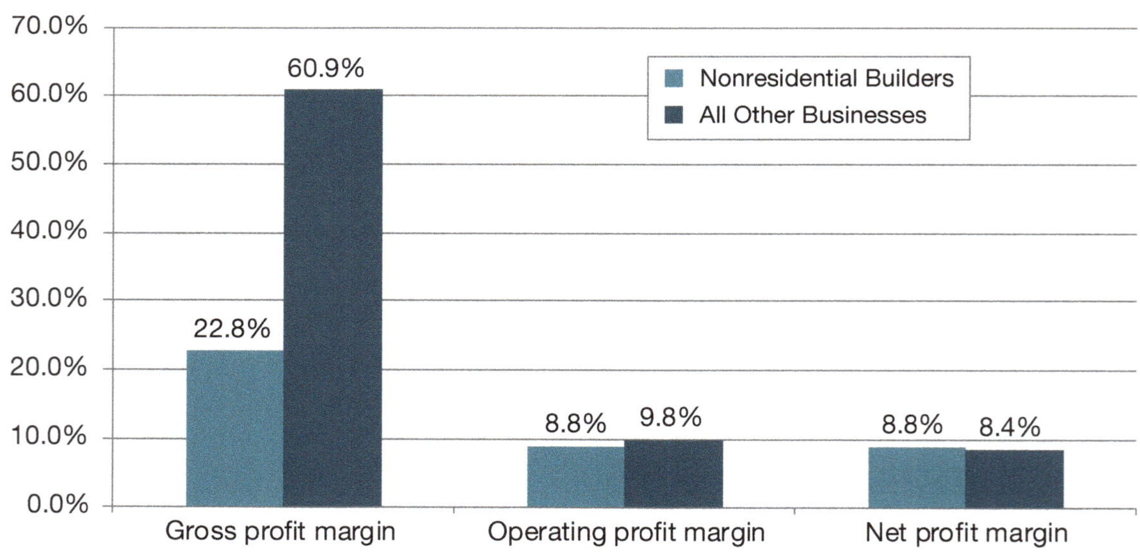

Gross profit margin = gross profit/revenue
Operating profit margin = operating profit/revenue
Net profit margin = net income/revenue

Profit margins. Nonresidential builders have lower median gross profit and operating profit margins than other businesses, according to data from DealStats. The gross profit margin for nonresidential builders is 22.8%, compared to 60.9% for all other businesses. The operating profit margin for nonresidential builders is 8.8%, compared to 9.8% for all other businesses. Conversely, the net profit margin for nonresidential builders is 8.8%, compared to 8.4% for all other businesses (see Exhibit 6).

Exhibits 7, 8, and 9 display the interquartile range of selling prices of nonresidential builders relative to other businesses. The interquartile range provides a measure of dispersion. Interquartile range is the difference between the 25th and 75th percentiles (also called the first and third quartiles), so the interquartile range describes the middle 50% of observations. The top of the orange rectangle indicates the 75th percentile, the bottom of the blue rectangle indicates the 25th percentile, and the line where the two rectangles meet represents the median. If the interquartile range is large, it means the middle 50% of observations are spaced

Exhibit 7. Selling Price/Revenue—Interquartile Range

	Nonresidential Builders	All Other Businesses
90th percentile	0.8	2.0
75th percentile	0.7	0.9
Median	0.4	0.5
25th percentile	0.2	0.3
10th percentile	0.1	0.2

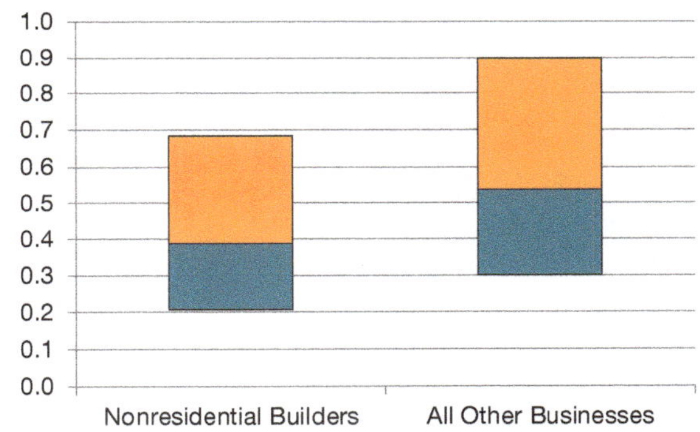

The graph displays the interquartile range. The blue rectangle indicates the spread between the first quartile (or 25th percentile) and the median, and the orange rectangle indicates the spread between the median and the third quartile (or 75th percentile).

Values over 100 have been eliminated.

Exhibit 8. Selling Price/SDE—Interquartile Range

	Nonresidential Builders	All Other Businesses
90th percentile	3.6	5.8
75th percentile	3.1	3.6
Median	2.7	2.5
25th percentile	1.7	1.6
10th percentile	1.5	1.1

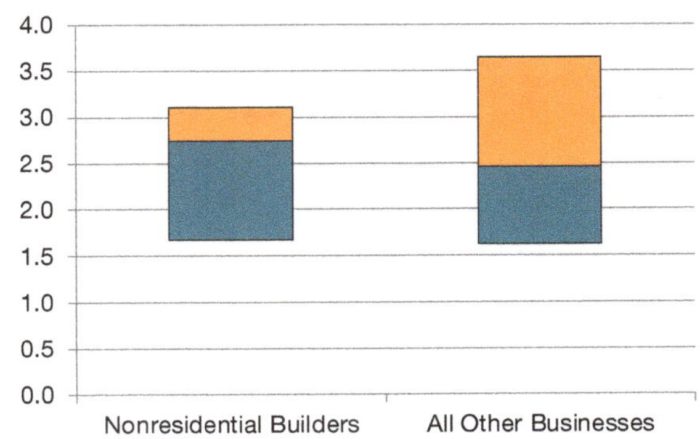

The graph displays the interquartile range. The blue rectangle indicates the spread between the first quartile (or 25th percentile) and the median, and the orange rectangle indicates the spread between the median and the third quartile (or 75th percentile).

SDE = seller's discretionary earnings
Values over 100 have been eliminated.

far apart, and, if the interquartile range is narrow, it means the middle 50% of observations are spaced close together.

Exhibit 9. Selling Price/EBITDA—Interquartile Range

	Nonresidential Builders	All Other Businesses
90th percentile	15.6	18.2
75th percentile	8.2	8.9
Median	4.3	4.2
25th percentile	3.1	2.2
10th percentile	1.6	1.3

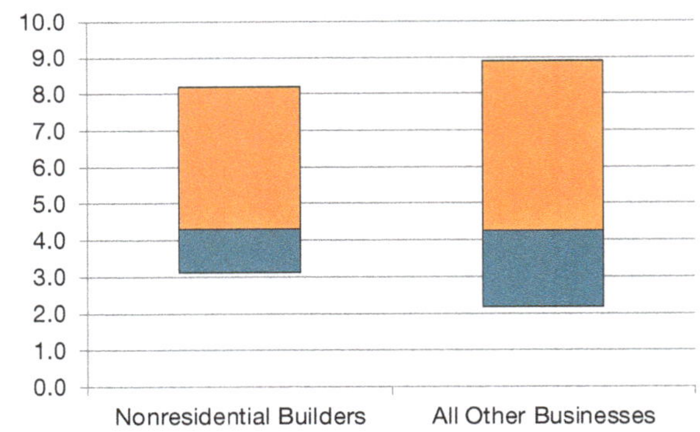

The graph displays the interquartile range. The blue rectangle indicates the spread between the first quartile (or 25th percentile) and the median, and the orange rectangle indicates the spread between the median and the third quartile (or 75th percentile).

EBITDA = earnings before interest, taxes, depreciation, and amortization
Values over 100 have been eliminated.

Exhibit 10. Operating Profit Margin—Interquartile Range

	Nonresidential Builders	All Other Businesses
90th percentile	19.3%	35.3%
75th percentile	12.3%	21.1%
Median	8.8%	9.8%
25th percentile	2.5%	1.9%
10th percentile	0.6%	-6.3%

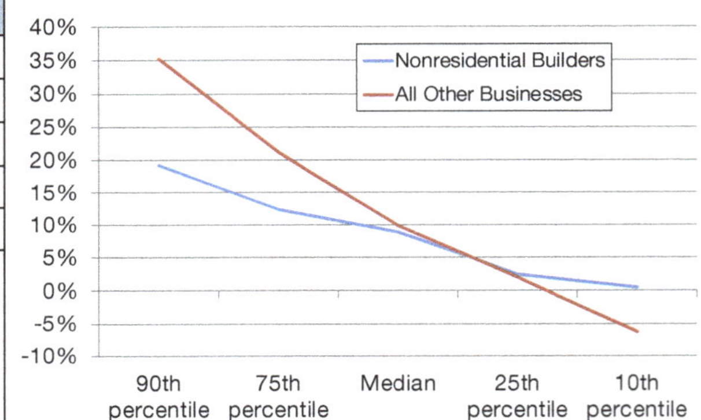

Exhibit 11. Net Profit Margin—Interquartile Range

	Nonresidential Builders	All Other Businesses
90th percentile	19.6%	34.1%
75th percentile	12.5%	19.9%
Median	8.8%	8.4%
25th percentile	3.2%	1.0%
10th percentile	0.9%	-8.0%

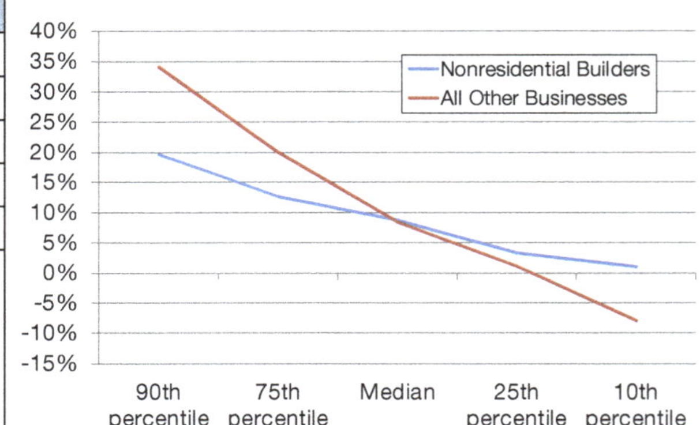

Operating and net profit margins are provided in Exhibits 10 and 11. The profit margins are plotted on the graphs by percentiles for both. The blue line represents the profit margins for nonresidential builders, while the red line represents all other businesses. The median (or the 50th percentile) is where the lines intersect and 50% of the observations have a higher value and 50% of the observations have a lower value. When reviewing the graphs, we see that the spread between the 10th percentile and the 90th percentile is less for nonresidential builders relative to all other businesses, so it appears there is less variability in profits for nonresidential builders relative to other businesses.

The median operating profit margin for nonresidential builders is 8.8%, lower than the 9.8% operating profit margin for other businesses.

The median net profit margin for nonresidential builders is 8.8%, compared with 8.4% for other businesses.

Median ratios are provided in Exhibit 12. The quick ratio measures a company's ability to meet its short-term obligations with its most liquid assets. The data indicate that nonresidential builders have a slightly higher quick ratio than other businesses in DealStats and therefore higher liquidity (1.2 versus 1.1). The return on equity ratio measures a business's profitability by displaying how much profit a company generates with the money shareholders have invested. The data indicate

Exhibit 12. Median Ratios

Median Liquidity Ratios

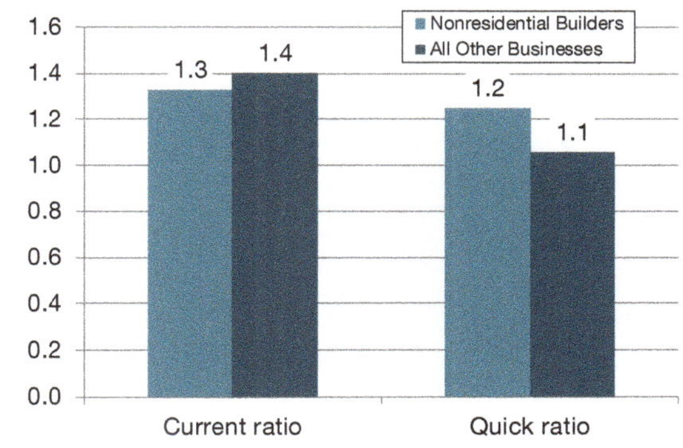

Median Profitability Ratios

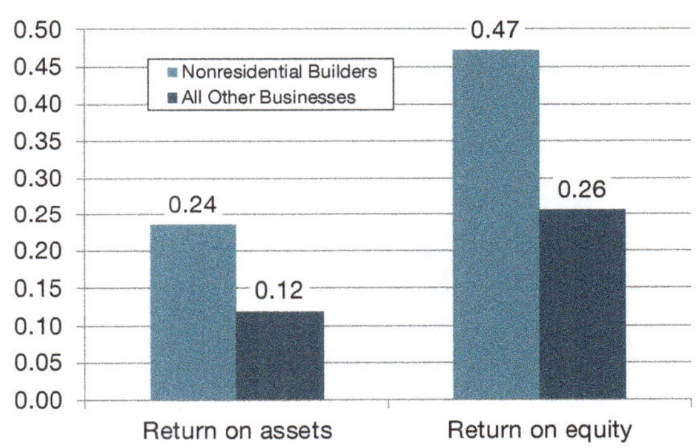

Median Activity Ratios

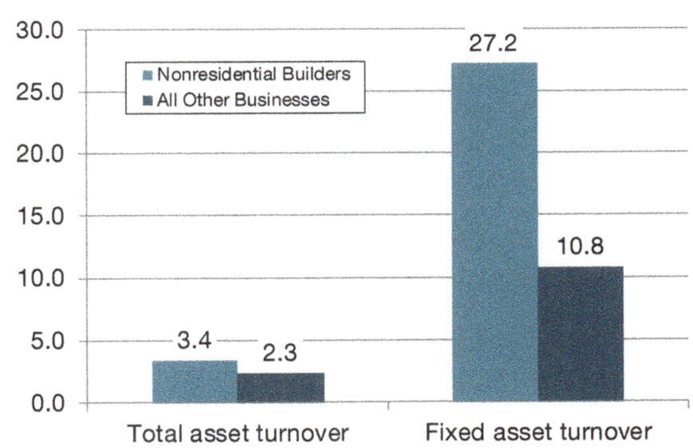

Current ratio = current assets/current liabilities
Quick ratio = (current assets - inventory)/current liabilities
Total asset turnover = revenue/total assets
Fixed asset turnover = revenue/fixed assets
Return on assets = net income/total assets
Return on equity = net income/equity

that nonresidential builders generate higher profits from equity investments than do other businesses (0.47 versus 0.26). The fixed-asset turnover ratio measures a business's ability to generate net sales from fixed-asset investments (specifically property, plant, and equipment, net of depreciation). Nonresidential builders generate almost triple the sales relative to fixed assets when compared to other businesses (27.2 versus 10.8).

11. Pricing Construction Companies: Rules of Thumb From the *Business Reference Guide*[1]

The information provided in this chapter is derived from the online version of the *Business Reference Guide (BRG)*, written and compiled by Thomas L. West. Despite caveats about using rules of thumb in pricing business, they are commonly used to do just that. They may supply a quick fix, but, if used properly, rules of thumb can come close to what the business will ultimately sell for, says West. The data below are current as of December 2019.

Rules of Thumb

- 20% to 30% of annual sales plus inventory;
- 1.5 times to 2.5 times seller's discretionary earnings plus inventory;
- 2 times to 3.5 times EBIT; and
- 2 times to 4 times EBITDA.

General Information

The following offer some observations from experts in the field who have been involved in the sale or valuation of a construction company.

- "A new owner needs sales skills for client acquisition, a license, project management skills (or hire a competent foreman and/or general manager), and operating capital sufficient to carry projects while awaiting progress payments."

1 The *Business Reference Guide* is available at bvresources.com/brg.

- "To operate a successful construction company, an owner needs the same skills any other business owner needs—the ability to manage, excellent bookkeeping habits, and commitment to market the business. Construction is an industry which heavily relies on skilled labor, so employing a good manager is key for growth. Too many newbie owners think they can manage people, generate business, monitor the work, and more. The truth is, in order to grow, an owner must learn to delegate tasks. The most successful businesses involve an owner who keeps an eye on things (especially financial) but doesn't get involved in the day-to-day operations."

- "Recurring revenue is the most important trend we see these days. Developing client loyalty through 'cell phone plan' models is a value driver."

- "A buyer of a construction company needs essentially two basic skills: the ability to run and manage a business, and an understanding of the trades. The first skill is by far the most crucial because if one does not understand the basics of running a business, no matter what the industry, he or she will likely fail. The owner must know accounting, payroll, insurance, contracts, etc. However, the second skill is also very important because one must know where to spend dollars to achieve the best results. For example, in construction, the look of the shop and office is probably far less crucial than the ability to generate accurate material estimates. Only an understanding of the specific trade of the business will ensure this."

- "Regarding licensing, different states require different things, but most require some sort of license or certification to do business. For the more stringent states, such as California, a buyer will need to investigate what is mandatory before buying a company, because some requirements might preclude an otherwise viable buyer."

- "A new owner needs the following:

    - **"Skills:** Project management, bookkeeping and accountancy, leadership, presenting, delegation, and sales;

    - **"Education:** High school or GED and a general or specialty contractor's license earned at the state level;

    - **"Experience:** General business and construction technology; and

    - **"Licensing:** Department of business and professional regulations of the state in which the business operates."

- "Find a special niche and earn higher margins and build an excellent reputation."

Expert Ratings

- Competition: 2.5 (0 = Low : 4 = High);
- Amount of risk: 2.1 (0 = Low : 4 = High);
- Historical profit trend: 2.9 (0 = Down : 4 = Up);
- Marketability: 2.5 (0 = Low : 4 = High);
- Industry trend: 3.1 (0 = Declining : 4 = Growing);
- Ease of replication: 1.7 (0 = Easy : 4 = Difficult); and
- Location and facilities: 2.5 (0 = Low : 4 = High).

Expert Comments

The following offer some further observations from experts in the field who have been involved in the sale or valuation of a construction company.

- "Advice for buyers: analyze financial and project trends carefully and over as long a time frame as possible."
- "Advice for sellers: build consistent revenues/profits with varied client/referral base; develop a tenured team (at least the key people)."
- "Licensing requirements tend to create barriers to entry. As a service business, margins tend to be strong, and with the exception of certain contractors who require heavy equipment, the capital needs tend to be minimal. A common challenge in this industry is hiring and retaining trade employees; successful contractors take care of their employees with generous benefits, i.e., vacation, company vehicle, holidays, medical reimbursement."
- "For a buyer, find a company with good books (this might be difficult). Construction companies are notorious for having messy and skewed books. For a seller, commit to keeping accurate financials. The extra money you might pay in taxes now will be dwarfed by what you will make when you sell—you will command a much higher price if your books are clean."

- "Construction, in general, is an easy industry to enter. This factor makes competition fierce. While a construction business can make a lot of money and make it quickly, there is significant risk because of how closely the industry follows the economy."
- "The strongest and most valuable businesses are those which have reliable management in place, high revenues, and repeat business."
- "Make yourself replaceable! Develop supervisory staff who are hungry to learn management and become company leaders."
- "Buyers should try to keep the seller involved for at least six months during the transition to turn over business relationships. Sellers can offer to qualify buyers for six months to a year for a fee. This opens up the buyer pool which is generally small due to the licensing needed to operate the business. A buyer can qualify for his or her own license during that time or hire a licensed manager."

Seller Financing

- "Acquisitions tend to be investor-operator funded, with some SBA financing. Most sellers don't offer seller financing—their motivation tends to be cash in the chips and move on."
- "Seller financing is a necessary part of most sales. Banks don't favor construction (because of its volatility) and are adverse to lending on a deal unless there is substantial value. Sellers also are often in a position where they will be qualifying a license for a buyer, so being close to the business for a time after the sale is common."
- "Ten percent down, 80% SBA, 10% seller note."
- "SBA financing is common, and some seller financing is used as an alternative. Mostly, seller financing is used to limit buyers' risk, so the loans are small and short term."

Questions to Ask Owners

- "How long will you stay on in a transition? Often, the seller is the key salesperson. How do they acquire new business? Do they have varied sources of referrals, or is it predominantly word of mouth? How much work is done with in-house tradesmen versus subcontractors?"
- "Are you willing to remain connected to the business for several months after the sale to assist in the transition (via a consulting agreement, or license qualification agreement)?"
- "What is your turnover rate? How has the opioid crisis affected your ability to hire? What's the longest vacation you've taken in recent years?"

- "What is your quick ratio? What is the percent of completion for each job? How much working capital does the business have in cash? Who are your major clients?"

Pricing Tips

- "The work in progress (WIP) is important to evaluating the continuity of the business, as well as aiding in confirming the value for pricing purposes. More important than in most business models, it is helpful to learn how construction-related businesses have weathered economic downturns, as these entities tend to closely follow economic cycles."
- "In my opinion, pricing a construction is one of the most difficult businesses to price. For one, there is extreme variety in how profit is calculated because construction is an industry where an owner can expense almost anything. You can look at two companies with similar work and similar revenues, and find a vast difference in how much profit they generate. Second, an owner's day-to-day involvement has a great bearing on value, in a buyer's mind. A company dependent upon an owner's personality, contacts, and reputation is considerably less valuable than a company independent of the owner."
- "Pricing is generally based on assets (fair market value), not including cash, receivables or investments. The best time to sell a construction business is, naturally, when it can command the highest price. Companies are worth more when they have been trading well and increasing profit in recent years, as well as demonstrating the potential for further growth."

Benchmark Data[2]

Statistics (Municipal Building Construction)

- Number of establishments: 45,397;
- Average profit margin: 3.5%;
- Revenue per employee: $1,185,000;
- Average number of employees: 3.7; and
- Average wages per employee: $63,851.

Products and Services Segmentation

- General contracting: 52.5%;

2 Data for Statistics, Products and Services Segmentation, Major Market Segmentation, Industry Costs, Market Share, and Employment Size used by permission IBISWorld, ibisworld.com.

- Construction management: 20.7%;
- Remodeling contracting: 15.6%; and
- Other construction activities: 11.2%.

Major Market Segmentation

- Educational building construction: 53.7%;
- Healthcare facilities construction: 24.3%;
- Recreational building construction: 15.0%;
- Public safety facilities construction: 5.3%; and
- Religious building construction: 1.7%.

Industry Costs

- Profit: 3.5%;
- Wages: 5.4%;
- Purchases: 48.2%;
- Depreciation: 0.4%;
- Marketing: 0.8%;
- Rent and utilities: 2.5%; and
- Other: 39.2%.

Other Metrics:

- Specialty contractors have much higher margins than a general contractor; and
- Many service-related contracting businesses will charge at least two times their direct costs as their hourly fee for service.

Industry Trends

- "Since these firms tend to be tied to economic cycles, a lot will depend on how the economy evolves. Residential construction will contract first, then commercial, and finally government."

- "[T]he seven biggest factors to watch this year[3]:
    - "Modular construction heights increasing;
    - "Technology is supplementing, not replacing, human workers;
    - "Design-build's popularity is growing;
    - "Building lean is cutting waste in all forms;
    - "More drones taking flight;
    - "Private firms are leading high-speed rail projects; and
    - "Gen Z is growing up."

Disadvantages

- "Feast or famine is the name of the game in this business. It's difficult to plan for the lean times when we are eating the fattened calf. Many construction companies crash and burn when the economy tanks because they get used to operating at high levels and can't adjust when business drops."
- "It is brutally hard to attract and retain talented help. Trade school grads are seeking top pay before earning by demonstrating loyalty and commitment."
- "Competition creates the need to continue aggressive marketing campaigns."
- "Ups and downs of economy, reliance upon employees and inconsistency."
- "Volatility due to mismanagement."
- "In business for yourself."
- "High bonding costs."
- "The main disadvantages of being in construction are the high risk factor and the dependence upon the general economy and home sales (this is not a recession-proof industry)."

---

3 Kim Slowey, Laurie Cowing, Joe Beeton, and Kathleen Brown, "7 Trends That Will Shape Commercial Construction in 2019," Jan. 7, 2019, constructiondive.com/news/7-trends-that-will-shape-commercial-construction-in-2019/543978.

- "High risk and high working-capital requirements. Many construction companies fail from lack of capital even though they are profitable."
- "People intensive. Material price volatility, seasonality."

Advantages

- "Satisfaction of project completion; good margins if operated properly."
- "Building is as crucial to the economy as food or real estate. It will never go away, as long as people live in houses or work in buildings. There's a built-in permanence to this industry."
- "High-end homeowners are done with opening, closing, and repairing machinery and equipment. Contractors are proving that this trend will carry them through the next economic downturn."
- "Recurring revenue from business relationships."
- "High profit potential, very satisfying work, and bettering communities."
- "There will be no other industry or sector that will experience the amount of growth in the next decades due to the replacement of infrastructure plus creation of new ones."
- "In business for yourself."
- "The main advantages of being in construction are the high potential for profitability and the ease of entry. Done properly, significant growth can happen fast."
- "As the general construction skill set of most people is diminishing over time, they will depend more on hiring out these trades. The handyman type business will be in greater demand and the tradespeople will be harder to find."
- "Cost of entry is low and net profit margins can be very high."
- "Construction companies can be very profitable and have made a lot of money for a lot of people."

12. Building Company Financial Metric and Business Model Resources

The editors at Business Valuation Resources have compiled a select list of free and fee-based industry resources, which are good to consult when researching the current state of the building industry as a whole, as well as valuation principles of different types of building company assets.

BUILDING INDUSTRY: SOURCES OF INFORMATION AND DATA

BizMiner

bvresources.com/bizminer

BizMiner offers extensive and cost-effective industry and geographic data. It covers 6,500 lines of business in thousands of U.S. market areas.

BizMiner's five-year financial statement analysis includes income statements, balance sheets, and key financial ratios, with data available by sales size range on a national, state, and metro area level. It provides:

- Income and expense detail in dollars and percentages;
- Balance sheets in dollars and percentages;
- Cash flow analysis;
- Liquidity and working capital ratios;
- Profitability and return on investment ratios;

- Asset turnover and efficiency ratios; and
- Capital structure and debt service ratios.

For information on construction contractors, search for NAICS code 23611 for residential construction and 236220 for nonresidential construction.

The *Business Reference Guide* (*BRG*)
bvresources.com/brg

BRG provides "rules of thumb" information on pricing construction companies, among hundreds of other industries. Also includes pricing tips from industry experts, benchmark information that provides comparison data, and interesting facts about many different businesses and industries.

DealStats
bvresources.com/dealstats

DealStats is a robust online database boasting the most complete financial details on thousands of acquired private companies, with nearly 200 data points per sale. With six valuation multiples and 13 financial ratios, each transaction includes detailed data vital to applying the market approach, deriving a selling price, benchmarking performance, or performing a fairness opinion analysis.

The detailed, transaction-by-transaction data on construction contractors can be purchased at bvresources.com/dealstats by searching SIC codes 1521 and 1522 for residential construction companies and 1541 and 1542 for nonresidential construction companies.

Dodge Data & Analytics
www.construction.com

Dodge Data & Analytics empowers its clients to better understand their markets, uncover key relationships, size growth opportunities, and pursue those opportunities with success.

***Economic Outlook Update* (*EOU*)**
bvresources.com/eou

EOU monthly and quarterly reports digest expansive research from the leading authoritative sources into one convenient and cost-effective report. Among other U.S. economic information, *EOU* includes data and trends associated with the U.S. housing and construction markets.

First Research
bvresources.com/firstresearch

First Research Industry Profiles provide detailed industry and economic analysis in thousands of segments to gain key insights into industry or geographic area. Reports are available on a subscription or single-report basis. Each industry profile includes important sections on:

- Critical issues;
- Quarterly industry update;
- Industry overview;
- Credit and business risk issues;
- Business trends; and
- Industry forecasts.

To find a First Research report on construction contractors, visit data.bvresources.com/FRProfilesSelectIndustry.asp and search SIC codes 1521 and 1522 for residential construction companies and 1541 and 1542 for nonresidential construction companies.

Vertical IQ Inc.
bvresources.com/verticaliq

Vertical IQ is a Raleigh, N.C.-based industry research solution with actionable content covering over 500 industries. Designed to help valuation practitioners, Vertical IQ profiles dive into the details of risks, trends, cash flow, operations, and financial challenges inherent to niche businesses of all types.

EDUCATIONAL RESOURCES

Valuing Residential and Commercial Builders
sub.bvresources.com/trainingeventpast.asp?WebinarID=666

A BVR webinar featuring Pasquale Rafanelli (Empire Valuation Consultants), which was presented on Oct. 30, 2018.

Valuing Construction Companies
sub.bvresources.com/bvstore/cd3.asp?pid=CD130

A BVR webinar featuring Don Drysdale (Drysdale Valuation PLLC) and M. Keith Prescott (Wisan, Smith, Racker & Prescott LLP), which was presented on May 13, 2010.

JOURNALS AND TRADE PUBLICATIONS

Builder Magazine is an online resource that provides business owners and managers with in-depth coverage of the construction industry: builderonline.com.

Constructor provides news, trends, and statistics from the Associated General Contractors of America: constructormagazine.com.

Construction Business Owner offers news and trends for construction business owners: constructionbusinessowner.com.

TRADE ASSOCIATIONS

Associated Builders and Contractors is a national construction industry trade association representing more than 21,000 members: abc.org.

Associated General Contractors of America represents more than 26,000 contractors, including over 6,500 of America's leading general contractors, and over 9,000 specialty-contracting firms: agc.com.

National Association of Home Builders is an association that represents the largest network of craftsmen, innovators, and problem solvers dedicated to building and enriching communities. Operating at the local, state, and national levels, the NAHB Federation helps its members gain a competitive advantage: nahb.org.

BVR
What It's Worth

bvresources.com

Trustworthy business valuations start here.

About Business Valuation Resources

Every informed stakeholder in business valuation, performance benchmarking, or risk assessment turns to Business Valuation Resources (BVR) for authoritative deal and market data, news and research, training, and expert opinion. Trust BVR for unimpeachable business valuation intelligence. BVR's data, publications, and analysis have won in the boardroom and the courtroom for over two decades.

Deal & Market Data

- DealStats
- Cost of Capital Professional
- Valuation Benchmarking Platform
- BIZCOMPS
- Economic Outlook Update
- FactSet Mergerstat/BVR Control Premium Study
- Stout Restricted Stock Study™
- Valuation Advisors Discount for Lack of Marketability Study
- ktMINE Royalty Rate Data & License Agreements
- First Research Industry, State & Province Profiles
- BizMiner Industry Financial Reports
- Mergerstat Review & Mergerstat Review Monthly
- Butler Pinkerton Calculator – Total Cost of Equity and Public Company Specific Risk Calculator
- Vertical IQ - U.S. and Canada Industry Profiles

News & Research

- BVResearch Pro
- Business Valuation Update
- BVLaw
- Economic Outlook Update
- Business Reference Guide Online

Guides, Books & Reports

- Digital Library
- Guides & Books
- Special Reports
- Legal Compendiums
- Yearbooks

Training & CPE

- Webinars
- Web Workshops & Special Series
- Desktop Learning Centers
- Self-study CPE
- eLearning courses

Learn more about all of our offerings at:
bvresources.com
Contact us at: 1-503-479-8200 or info@bvresources.com

www.ingramcontent.com/pod-product-compliance
Lightning Source LLC
LaVergne TN
LVHW070107021026
849160LV00026B/1700